CAMBRIDGE

Hobson's Conduit on the Market Hill, from J. J. Smith's **The Cambridge Portfolio,** *1840*

F. A. Reeve

CAMBRIDGE

B. T. Batsford Ltd
London

First published 1976

Copyright F. A. Reeve 1976
Printed in Great Britain by The Pitman Press
Bath for the
publishers B. T. Batsford Ltd
4 Fitzhardinge Street, London W1H OAH

ISBN 0 7134 3225 X

Contents

Acknowledgments

The Author and Publishers would like to thank Cambridge University Press for the use of plate 6 and Bowes & Bowes (Cambridge) Ltd for the jacket illustration.

Illustrations

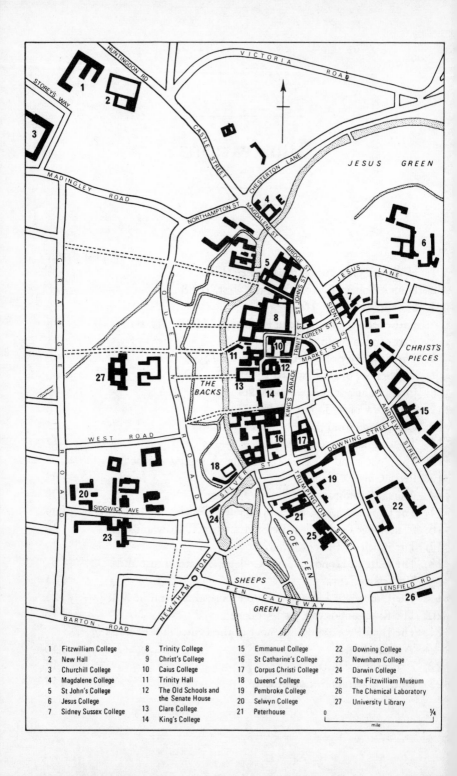

1	Fitzwilliam College	8	Trinity College	15	Emmanuel College	22	Downing College
2	New Hall	9	Christ's College	16	St Catharine's College	23	Newnham College
3	Churchill College	10	Caius College	17	Corpus Christi College	24	Darwin College
4	Magdalene College	11	Trinity Hall	18	Queens' College	25	The Fitzwilliam Museum
5	St John's College	12	The Old Schools and the Senate House	19	Pembroke College	26	The Chemical Laboratory
6	Jesus College	13	Clare College	20	Selwyn College	27	University Library
7	Sidney Sussex College	14	King's College	21	Peterhouse		

0 ¼
mile

ONE

From Early Times
to the First Colleges

The dates when students first appeared in Oxford and Cambridge are uncertain, but it is known that by 1200 there was, at Oxford, a group of scholars organized on the lines of the university of Paris. There may also have been teachers and students in Cambridge by this time. In 1209, during one of the frequent disturbances, a townswoman of Oxford was killed, allegedly by students. The mayor and burgesses, finding that those believed to be responsible had fled, seized hostages, and King John gave the townsmen leave to execute them. The other students took fright and many left Oxford for Reading, Paris, and Cambridge.

Those who arrived in Cambridge found a town much older than Oxford. There had been an unfortified Belgic settlement on the high ground at Castle Hill, probably abandoned in A.D. 43, when a Roman fort was established. To the north stretched the undrained Fenlands. Drainage has so transformed the fen country in modern times, that it is difficult to imagine it as it was. Rivers taking the rainfall of the central counties poured their waters into a vast area towards the Wash, creating swamps intersected by numerous streams and lakes, with large quantities of reed and sedge, and copses of willows.

To the south-west, the upland country of boulder clay was covered with dense forest. The fens and the forests formed a barrier between East Anglia and the rest of the country, and there was only a narrow corridor through which travellers could pass. In the middle of this neck of land was Cambridge, with its river which could be crossed by ford or boat. It is believed that a wooden bridge came into existence between 731 and 875. The Roman commanders must have recognised that the high ground to the west of the river was a suitable place to control a river crossing of strategic importance.

There were civilians on the hillside by A.D. 70, and as their number increased, their huts of timber and daub, with clay or cement floors, tiled hearths and roofs, gradually extended to the present sites of Magdalene and Sidney colleges, and towards Madingley Road. The Romans eventually had a large rectangular enclosure of about 28 acres, replaced in the second century by a town with a grid system of streets. In the middle of the fourth century, defensive walls 9 feet thick, backed by an earth rampart 30 feet wide with a ditch on the outside, were constructed. This little town flourished from 350-400 and into the fifth century, but was gradually deserted.

Several Roman roads passed through or close to Cambridge. The Via Devana from Colchester crossed the river near Magdalene bridge and continued to Godmanchester. Further west was Ermine Street, entering the county at Royston, with Akeman Street branching off at Wimpole Lodge and proceeding via Barton and Cambridge to Ely and Littleport. Remains of the Roman causeway between the Great Bridge and the Round Church were discovered in 1823 when an excavation was being made for the construction of a sewer. It was well-preserved, and formed of wooden piles supporting squared beams. The fact that this causeway was 14 feet below the present surface, shows how considerably the ground there has been raised through the centuries.

Romanised Britons were replaced by Anglo-Saxon invaders; the Danes wintered in the town in 875 and burnt it in 1010. In the tenth and early eleventh centuries, Cambridge was an important place at the head of a river having access to the sea through King's Lynn, and on the chief line of communication between East Anglia and the rest of England. There were wharves on the east bank near the church of St Clement, and the townsfolk became sufficiently wealthy to build the church of St Bene't in about 1025. Its original Anglo-Saxon tower is still standing, and is the oldest building in the town.

Houses were built on small ridges of gravel which provided a dry site, whereas all of the ground near the east side of the river, and the west side except the high ground north of the river crossing, was liable to be flooded. Visitors are puzzled to find that Market Hill, Peas Hill, etc., are no higher than the adjacent areas. The word Hill is ancient Cambridge usage to denote an open space which elsewhere would be called a Place or Square. In Norwich, the word Plain denotes similar open spaces.

There were a number of fraternities or guilds, each member making payments towards the maintenance of the society. Guilds were formed in those lawless times for mutual protection and assistance. To some extent they were religious societies, and attached to particular churches. Priests were paid to pray for the health and prosperity of members, and for their souls when they had died. They expended a great deal on lights for the churches, and members often bequeathed rents of property to pay for lights. Some people resented having to pay these 'candle-rents'.

After the Norman Conquest, King William destroyed 27 houses to build a castle, probably of wood, which served as a base for his military operations against the Saxon prelates and noblemen who, with Hereward, held out for some time at Ely. His sheriff, Picot, became a severe ruler of the shire. Near the castle Picot established the church of St Giles, and accommodation for six canons. His successor removed the canons in 1112 to a site at Barnwell, just outside the town, and Barnwell Priory, a house of Augustinian Canons, became of great importance throughout the Middle Ages. Richard II lodged there and held a parliament in 1388.

St Radegund's, a house of Benedictine nuns, was later established, and their fine church and buildings were to form the nucleus of Jesus College. Groups of houses arose adjacent to these two religious foundations. St Andrew the Less was presumably built to serve the people living near Barnwell Priory, and those near St Radegund's used the nave of the nuns' church.

The Church of the Holy Sepulchre, more commonly called the Round Church, the oldest of the four round churches in England, was consecrated in 1107, and is probably the oldest crusading church in the world. It closely resembles the Church of the Resurrection in Jerusalem, and must have been built by persons interested in or connected with the crusades. In 1135 Henry Frost, a rich burgess, founded the Hospital of St John, to be conducted by a small community of Augustinian canons to say masses and to care for the poor and infirm. In 1174 most of the town was destroyed by fire; Holy Trinity Church suffered complete destruction, and other churches, then built of wood, were damaged.

In the twelfth century, Cambridge became of increased importance as a commercial centre, and Sturbridge Fair attained international fame. King

John granted the fair in 1210-11 to a Leper Hospital founded in the middle of the twelfth century on a site beyond Barnwell Priory. The small Norman chapel survives. Leprosy was then prevalent due to the confined and dirty state of dwellings, and a deficiency of vegetables and fresh meat. Most of our vegetables, except onions, peas and beans, were unknown in medieval times. Sea fish, salted for preservation, was bought at Sturbridge Fair for winter meals. The monastic houses dug ponds for breeding freshwater fish, and remains of these survive in several college grounds.

The jurisdiction of the town was vested in the king himself, who was more inclined to delegate authority to the burgesses, whereas towns controlled by feudal lords or ecclesiastical bodies had a longer struggle to achieve independence. The first step towards emancipation occurred when the burgesses persuaded the sheriff to accept a fixed sum as the contribution of the town towards the royal exchequer. The next aim was to gain permission to pay direct to the king. A petition to Henry I was successful, and a charter gave the borough a monopoly of the trade of the county, and its own judicature.

Two charters of King John in 1201 and 1207 gave the guild merchants exemption from tolls on crossing rivers or bridges or on selling goods in all the king's lands except London, and the exclusive right of trading within the borough. The second charter provided, among other things, that 'The Burgesses shall have and hold the aforesaid town, with all its appurtenances, well and peaceably, freely and quietly, entirely, fully, and honourably in meadows and pastures, mills, pools and waters, with all their liberties and free customs. We grant also to them that they shall make of theselves a Provost (or Reeve), whom they will and when they will!'

Until about 1200 the principal officers of the town were four bailiffs. One of them took precedence and was later called the Mayor. It is believed that the first Mayor was Hervey fitzEustace of the Dunning family, one of the richest in Cambridge, and that he was of knightly rank. He lived in the stone building called The School of Pythagoras at a time when only a few people were wealthy enough to own a stone house. This was particularly true in Cambridge, as no good building stone is found in the vicinity, and houses were of timber and thatch. The School of Pythagoras still stands in the grounds of St John's, and there can be few towns where the house of its first Mayor still exists after eight centuries.

Cambridge east of the river was never fortified with a wall, but by the King's Ditch which left the river at the end of Mill Lane, crossed the present New Museums site to the front of Christ's, through the grounds of Sidney, to rejoin the river near the former electricity works. The date of construction is uncertain, but Henry III improved it in 1267 when trouble threatened from men of the Isle of Ely: 'He had gates made and ditches dug round the town with much diligence, nor would he allow the labourers to rest on holy days.' The gates were probably toll gates rather than defences.

The scholars who arrived in 1209 found a small but thriving town mainly within the boundary of the King's Ditch. Where the southern end of the ditch left the river stood two ancient mills, the King's Mill and the Bishop's Mill, and Milne Street ran from near the mills, parallel to the High Street, to a point near the Queen's Gate of Trinity. Lanes led from Milne Street to a number of hythes.

In Roman and Saxon times, there had been no direct route to London. Travellers then joined the Icknield Way at Royston, went on to meet the Ermine Street at Dunstable, and continued through St Albans. The town was surrounded by the common pastures, largely liable to be flooded, and by arable fields which were cultivated in narrow strips, though these were sometimes merged and some people owned comparatively large areas.

County landowners had to pay to maintain the bridge, and the sheriff was responsible for ensuring that it was kept in good repair, but he often failed to do so. Those liable to pay pontage rates objected to being obliged to contribute because they maintained that the bridge mainly benefited the town, and until the middle of the eighteenth century there were constant difficulties in collecting the money due.

*   *   *

The medieval students were often only 14 or 15 years old, and at first they lodged with the townsfolk. Soon they began to hire houses which became known as hostels, and later it became compulsory that a Master should be in charge. Fuller states that in 1280 there were 34 hostels, and also several inns occupied by scholars. By 1220-30 the Cambridge schools were important, as we know from contemporary documents and

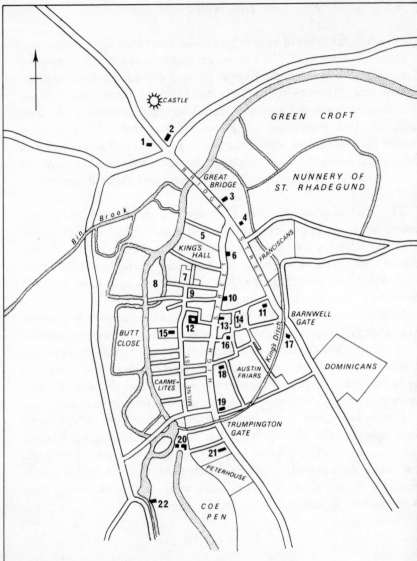

Cambridge before the foundation of the colleges

1	St Peter's Church	9	Gonville Hall	17	St Andrew's Church
2	St Giles' Church	10	St Michael's Church	18	St Bene't Church
3	St Clement's Church	11	Holy Trinity Church	19	St Botolph's Church
4	St Sepulchre's Church	12	The Schools	20	The King's and Bishop's Mills
5	St John's Hospital	13	Great St Mary's Church	21	Little St Mary's Church
6	All Saints' Church	14	The Market Place	22	Newnham Mill
7	Michaelhouse	15	St John Zachery's Church		
8	Garret Hostel Green	16	St Edward's Church		

0   ¼
mile

the fact that the king was often involved in the affairs of the university. The head of the university was the Chancellor, elected annually for about 300 years, and until 1482 always resident. The majority of the teachers were ecclesiastics, and most of the students were intended for the church. Two Proctors were elected annually to control finances, the sale of foodstuffs, and to punish offending students. A Master of Glomery supervised those who took only the grammar course with a view to becoming schoolmasters.

Manuscripts were scarce, and teaching was by lectures, the manuscripts being read slowly so that students could write down a great deal. The pupils sat on the floor covered with straw or rushes, with their hand-copied Latin grammars and texts, taking notes on oblong wooden tablets covered with black or green wax, and using a stylus of bone, ivory or metal. Latin was the language of the church and the learned, and all instruction was given in that tongue. Lectures were given in hired houses, and for about 200 years the university did not build anything for this purpose. In the thirteenth century more manuscripts became available. It took about fifteen months to make a copy of the Bible.

Many religious houses were established in the town. The black-robed Dominican or Preaching Friars first came to England in 1221, the Franciscans, in coarse grey gowns with a girdle of rope, in 1224. The latter arrived in Cambridge in 1225, and for 40 years occupied the house of Benjamin the Jew beside the Guildhall, until they began to build on the site of what is now Sidney Sussex College. Their monastery was surrounded by a wall extending from the entrance to Sussex Street, down that street to King Street and along the back of Malcolm Street, then along Jesus Lane. By 1279 this site was six acres in extent.

By 1238 the Dominicans were building on the site later taken over for Emmanuel. Both were teaching orders, playing a leading part in European universities. The Carmelites first settled in Chesterton in 1248, then removed to Newnham, where they built a handsome church, cloister, dormitory, and other buildings. In this church, Sir Simon Stock, the most celebrated General of the Order, saw a vision of the Virgin Mary. In 1292 they moved to the other side of the river because winter floods often prevented access to the town. They obtained leave to enclose within walls a plot of land between Milne Street and the river, provided that they made two doors through which defenders could pass at need.

The boys who came to study were ill-disciplined and high-spirited, difficult to control in the narrow streets and lanes, and there were frequent affrays with the townspeople, especially after kings began to give special privileges to the university. The inhabitants must often have felt like citizens of a town on whom alien troops had been billeted. In 1231, when the university authorities found it difficult to maintain order, the king issued four writs, decreeing that troublesome and rebellious clerks should be reported by the Chancellor and Masters to the Bishop of Ely, who could require the sheriff to imprison them in the castle, though he had to consult the university about punishments. It was also decreed that all students must be under the control of a Master.

In an attempt to remedy complaints of overcharging for rents and food, four officials called Taxors, two Masters and two townsmen, were appointed to supervise the markets and assess rents. The amusements of the citizens were curtailed by Henry III in 1245, when tournaments and tilting were prohibited within five miles of Cambridge because the crowds and noise disturbed studies.

There were frequent fights between students from the north and those from the south, and in 1261 townsfolk were involved, houses were raided and university records burnt. The disturbance was so serious that the king referred the matter to three Justices, and 16 townsmen were executed.

The open common fields were divided by the river into the West (or Cambridge) Field and the East (or Barnwell) Field. In the thirteenth century the trade of the town was expanding. It was the only place of any size in the county, and was a distribution centre for the products of the countryside such as meat, hides, corn, fish and flax, also reeds and sedge used for building and fuel, some of which was sent to London and abroad. Surplus corn was being exported to Ireland and Norway by the end of the twelfth century.

The rise in the price of corn benefited the whole county and the townsmen who owned strips in the arable fields. There was an increase in the number of craftsmen working in the town who could exchange their goods for the products of the countryside.

The castle was improved by Henry III in the 1260s, and Edward I made major changes from 1284, stone coming from Peterborough and Barnack. In 1295 about 100 men were at work, and a great hall of three storeys was built, also a large gatehouse and a curtain wall with four

owers. From 1295 the town was represented in Parliament by two
ourgesses who were paid a shilling a day while they were away from the
own. Until 1625 the M.P.s were chosen by a small number of the
ourgesses, usually eight.

* * *

A charter granted to the university in 1267-8 stipulated that two
aldermen and four of the more discreet and lawful burgesses should assist
he mayor and bailiffs to preserve the king's peace, and to search for
malefactors and receivers. Every parish had to elect two men who once a
ortnight would enquire whether any suspected person lodged there. The
charter provided for testing the weight and quality of bread and beer, and
ordered that the town should be kept clean. Two burgesses from every
treet were to be sworn in before the mayor to cleanse the town ditch.

In 1270 the town and the university assumed joint responsibility for
maintaining order, and 10 burgesses and 10 scholars were appointed at
an annual meeting summoned by the Vice-Chancellor called the Black
Assembly, because on these occasions he wore a black robe. This
additional indication of the influence of the university angered the
ownsfolk. In 1276 the Bishop of Ely ruled that the town clergy were
answerable to the Archdeacon, but that priests studying in the university
were subject to the Chancellor.

The course of study lasted for seven years, though not all of the
students remained for the full period. It embraced the seven liberal arts —
liberal because they were not intended as a help towards making money.
The initial course, the Trivium, consisted of grammar, rhetoric and logic.
Grammar embraced linguistics, writing, spelling, composition and general
literature. Rhetoric taught the craft of speech, and included a course in
letter-writing. As no printed books were available, a man who wished to
influence others had to be a persuasive speaker. Logic taught clear
thinking, leaning heavily on the works of Aristotle.

The Trivium was followed by the Quadrivium — arithmetic, geometry,
astronomy and music. Arithmetic included the use of the abacus and the
properties of numbers. The clumsy Roman numbers had been superseded
by Arabic numerals which had made rapid computation possible.
Geometry consisted mainly of Euclid's first book. Astronomy, then a

mixture of astrology and primitive science, was the most popular subject
There was little accurate scientific knowledge; students were taught that
ostriches eat iron, that elephants fear only dragons and mice, and that
weasels are conceived by the ear and delivered through the mouth.

In 1280 Hugh de Balsham, Bishop of Ely, placed some secular
scholars in the Hospital of St John, but the experiment was not successful
and in 1284 he removed them to two houses beyond St Peter's Church
They occupied these houses for 130 years, but when the Bishop died in
1286 he left money with which the scholars purchased more land and
erected a dining hall. Though much restored, parts of the original building
survive; students have taken meals in this hall for nearly 700 years. For
their devotions they used the adjacent church of St Peter.

The statutes of this first college made provision for a Master and 14
Fellows, and 40 years elapsed before the second Cambridge college was
founded. In the meantime more religious orders settled in the town.
including the Austin Friars, who occupied a site to the east of the church
of St Bene't. For more than 200 years after the foundation of Peterhouse.
only a minority of the teachers and students lived in a college.

In 1305 the Chancellor was empowered to summon townsmen, and
could imprison in the castle any layman convicted of assaulting a scholar.
A university charter of 1317 ordered that the Mayor and bailiffs, on
taking office, must swear an oath that they would maintain the privileges
of the university. This caused much resentment, and in 1322 scholars and
their hostels were attacked during a riot. A Papal Bull of 1318 decreed
that Cambridge should be a Studium Generale, no longer under the
jurisdiction of the bishop, and the Chancellor could exercise the powers of
absolution and excommunication. Henceforth, doctors of the university
might lecture in any christian land.

In 1323 Hervey de Stanton, Chancellor of the Exchequer to Edward
II, purchased a large house and founded Michaelhouse for a Master and
seven scholars. He also secured the advowson of St Michael's Church.
which he rebuilt with a large choir for his scholars, the remainder for the
parishioners.

Since at least 1317, Edward II had made provision for 12 boys from
the Chapel Royal to attend the university, and in 1336 Edward III
purchased a large house which stood on the present grass plot near Trinity
Chapel, to accommodate 32 scholars. King's Hall, of two storeys and

thatched, later occupied three sides of a small quadrangle. The number of chambers was increased in 1344, and later a brewhouse, bakehouse and granary were added. Both Michaelhouse and King's Hall were absorbed by Trinity when that college was founded by Henry VIII.

Most of the early colleges were founded to provide accommodation and a small stipend for teachers, and King's Hall was the first college in either Oxford or Cambridge to also admit undergraduates. The statutes forbade them to frequent taverns, introduce dogs, wear short swords or peaked shoes, and to use bows or catapults. Most of the inhabitants of Cambridge obtained water from wells or pumps, but in 1327 the Franciscans brought water in lead pipes from a spring off the Madingley Road to their monastery.

In 1326 the university obtained a royal licence to place scholars in two houses in Milne Street. University College was renamed Clare Hall twelve years later when it was refounded by Lady Elizabeth de Clare, a granddaughter of Edward I. Pembroke Hall was founded in 1347 by the Countess of Pembroke, and Gonville Hall in the same year by Edmund Gonville. The original site of the latter was in Free School Lane, but when the founder died in 1351 he left money with which his executor, William Bateman, Bishop of Norwich, acquired a new site at the corner of Milne Street and St Michael's Lane.

The parish church of St Peter had partly fallen down by about 1340, and a new church dedicated to the Virgin Mary took its place. The Black Death, which first appeared in England in 1348, had caused a serious shortage of clergy trained in canon and civil law. Of the 648 clergy in the diocese of Ely, at least 350 perished; almost everyone in the part of Cambridge near the castle died, and the remainder moved away. To fill some of the vacant posts for lawyers, Bishop Bateman founded the College of the Scholars of the Holy Trinity of Norwich, or Trinity Hall, in a hostel previously used by monks of Ely at the university.

The method for the election of the Town Council was prescribed in 1344, though it is possible that the existing scheme was merely being confirmed. The Council, known as the Four-and-Twenty, was to be elected by one man appointed by the outgoing Mayor and Council, and another by the commonalty. With few differences, the Council continued to be so elected until the Municipal Reform Act of 1835. It obtained its revenue by taxes on houses and land, customs on all goods brought into the town, the rents of market booths, fees for the admission of freemen, and court fines. By the middle of the fourteenth century the town had secured municipal independence, though limited by certain privileges enjoyed by the university.

The next college to be founded is unique because, in 1352, it was established by townsmen belonging to the Guilds of Corpus Christi and of the Blessed Virgin Mary, on a site beside St Bene't's. When, by about 1378, the Old Court was completed, it was the first closed quadrangle, and although some alterations have been made, it gives a present-day visitor a good impression of the appearance of a medieval college court.

For a long time the interior walls were not plastered, the floor was of stone or clay and covered with rushes, there were no ceilings to the upper floors, and the small windows were of oiled parchment with wooden shutters. At this time, some glass came from abroad, but it was seldom used even in the houses of the wealthy.

The Regent Masters continued to lecture in hired rooms until the Divinity School, built of stone rubble and begun in about 1350, was completed about 50 years later. The upper floor was a meeting place, later called the Regent House. Some of the students dressed more like soldiers than priests, in brightly coloured cloaks, and carried weapons, and in 1342 Archbishop Stratford issued an order that no student might receive any ecclesiastical degree or honour unless he reformed his person and apparel. The Carmelites or Whitefriars and the Gilbertine canons had white cloaks, the latter with sheepskin capes; the Dominicans, the canons of St John and St Giles, and the Benedictines were in black; the Austin Friars were dressed as hermits; and the Franciscans, in their coarse grey tunics, looked like peasants.

At a time when most students had to find lodgings either in private houses or in hostels, the monastic orders had erected well-equipped buildings, and many boys of 14 or 15 were induced to enter one of these. To counteract the influence of the monks and friars, the first English college of Walter de Merton at Oxford had excluded all members of the religious orders. Throughout the fourteenth century there were conflicts with the friars because they played an important part in teaching, but were not completely subject to university regulations. A statute forbade boys under 18 to enter a religious order, but this was revoked in 1366. Hugh de Balsham, who had founded Peterhouse, was a Benedictine monk, an order which imposed a less demanding and ascetic discipline than that of the mendicants.

The Masters were divided into two groups, the Regents and the Non-Regents. The Regent Masters were those who taught and lectured, and at first they possessed all the powers, but gradually the Non-Regents, who were graduates administering colleges, hostels, or religious societies, claimed more rights, and it was agreed that statutes had to be approved by a majority of both Regents and Non-Regents.

During the fourteenth century the town was less prosperous. There were frequent outbreaks of plague, especially in 1349, 1361, and 1369. By 1377 the population was about 3,000; owing to the ravages of the plague, the population of the whole country was only about two-thirds of the figure reached in the 1340s. Foul Lane, crossing what is now the Great Court of Trinity, was aptly named, and in 1393 it was said that many scholars fell sick because it stank so abominably.

The colleges were very humble institutions and for centuries the medieval students had to live in unheated rooms with floors of stone and unplastered walls. Numbed fingers must often have turned the pages of the heavy chained books in the libraries. Books were scarce and expensive, and the opportunity to use a library was one of the chief benefits of residence in a college. The hostels were more comfortable, and most of the wealthier young men lodged in these. In the colleges, a small body of men, sometimes less than a score, were closely associated as they studied, prayed and ate together. Having almost no links with the outside world, the members developed a very strong corporate feeling.

Through the centuries a host of benefactors left to the colleges money and estates, plate and books. Some of the donors were wealthy nobles, bishops, or merchants; others were former students, poor priests who could give no more than a single book. What did Gonville Hall, on its cramped site, do with 'seven score ewes and three score lambs . . . to be delyvered to the sayde master and felowes at midsomer,' given by the Lestrange family of Norfolk?

The scholars needed a large hall for some of their ceremonies, and from the earliest days of the university they met in Great St Mary's church. Throughout the Middle Ages, the naves of churches had no seating except a few movable benches, and they were used for secular purposes. There is no record of any formal agreement between the university and the parishioners, but in later years the university claimed that it had a right to use the church. By 1303 university sermons were being preached there.

When colleges built their own chapels, these too were used for meetings, disputations, lectures, and even plays, until the end of the seventeenth century. When Queen Elizabeth visited Cambridge in 1564, a play by Plautus was performed in Latin in the antechapel of King's on a stage extending across the whole width of the west end. Great St Mary's was rebuilt largely through funds raised by the university, and on one occasion the Proctors travelled about the country for 20 days to solicit money.

*   *   *

During the Peasants' Revolt of 1381, rioters destroyed the houses of a landowner and of William Wigmore, an Esquire Bedell, then attacked Corpus, burnt its books and charters, and sacked houses belonging to burgesses and university property. Although Corpus had been founded by townsmen, the college had become unpopular because it owned more property than any other, and because half of the houses in the town had to pay 'candle rents', the tax originally intended to pay for lights at guild services, but now used by the college for other purposes.

The display of wealth during the annual Corpus Christi processions may also have caused resentment. This procession was headed by the aldermen of the guild, and men carrying enamelled silver shields with coats of arms and symbols of the Passion. Next came the Master of Corpus beneath a canopy, bearing the Host in a valuable silver-gilt tabernacle, the Vice-Chancellor, the Fellows and Scholars of Corpus and members of the university, the Mayor, the Town Council, burgesses and many ordinary citizens, all carrying torches. The procession went from the college to the Great Bridge and all parts of the town.

In the past 100 years, eight colleges owning much property had been established, and the rioters of 1381 had grievances not only against landlords and government officials, but also against the university. On the second day of rioting a mob seized jewels and vessels at Great St Mary's, broke open the university chest, and burnt its muniments. The Mayor and bailiffs forced the university and college authorities to sign deeds in which they renounced all royal privileges granted to them, and promised to conform to the law and custom of the Borough. University charters and deeds were burnt in the market.

On the following day, Barnwell Priory was attacked by a mob of 1,000 men who broke down walls enclosing former common land, and the riots were not suppressed until the Bishop of Norwich entered Cambridge with a body of armed men.

The Mayor and bailiffs were summoned to Westminster, and the deeds which the university authorities had been forced to sign were cancelled. The king increased the farm of the town and took away its franchises. They were restored a year later, but the university was given jurisdiction over the buying and selling of food and drink. These disorders and their aftermath embittered relations between the town and the university for generations, and the supervision of trade in particular caused disputes until 1856.

Fuller gives the following account of relations between the university and the town in 1384:

'First. That hereafter the oversight of all victuals should belong to the Chancellor; so that no townsman ever since putteth a crumb of bread or a drop of beer into his mouth, but what first is weighed and measured by an officer of the University.
Secondly. That the Chancellor and the University should have power to set prices on candles (very necessary, I assure you, to hard students) and to license all victualling-houses, and oversee all wares and weights at Sturbridge Fair.
Thirdly. That no action be brought by any townsman against Scholar or Scholar's servant save only in the Court of the Chancellor.
Fourthly. That the University have power to punish and amerce all forestallers, regrators &c paying a rent of ten pounds a year for that privilege into the Exchequer; this their power extending to the town and suburbs thereof. We must not forget that all kinds of fuel, wood, coals, turf &c were then subjected to the Chancellor, as to set the price thereof.'

A serious fire of 1385 destroyed more than 100 houses, and in the following year the Guildhall or Tolbooth, originally a place for weighing goods brought to market, in order to levy tolls, was rebuilt. The first building was only a roof supported on pillars, but now an upper storey, with a hall, an aldermen's parlour, a kitchen and pantry, was added. The walls were covered with hangings, and the charters and other muniments were kept in a chest.

The first English Sanitation Act was that of a Parliament held in Cambridge in 1388, and was probably prompted by the filthy state of the town. In addition to the Great Bridge there were bridges over two distinct branches of the river at Small Bridges (Silver Street), one on the site of the present bridge, and the other over a branch of the river coming from Newnham Mill. The ditch bordering Queens' Grove is all that remains of this river.

These wooden bridges and the road were maintained by a hermit. On a small island behind Newnham Grange he tended a chapel licensed by the Bishop of Ely in 1396. Three years later, the bridges and causeway being unsafe so that accidents frequently happened to persons and carriages, Henry IV sent greetings to John Laye, the hermit, and gave him leave to levy customs for the repair of the Small Bridges and the causeway. In 1401-02 carts shod with iron wheels were forbidden to cross, and in 1428 all the willows in the vicinity were reserved for the hermit to be used for the repair of the road.

In 1428 the Benedictines secured two houses for the accommodation of monks attending the university, and in later years a number of houses of the Order built Buckingham (later Magdalene) College. In the same year, King's Hall began to build King Edward's Tower, the first example of the monumental gateways of several Cambridge colleges. Godshouse, for training grammar school masters, was founded in 1439 by William Byngham, a London parish priest, but it was soon removed when its site was required for King's College.

TWO

The Later Middle Ages, 1440-1550

In 1441 Henry VI, then only nineteen, decided to build a college for a Rector and twelve scholars, and obtained a garden, only 40 by 25 yards, behind the partly built Old Schools. Additional land was bought in 1443, but the site was still small. Building began, including a chapel which fell down in 1537. The king had already founded Eton College, and he decided to enlarge his original plans so that scholars from Eton could continue their studies in Cambridge.

The revised scheme envisaged magnificent buildings for a Provost, 70 scholars, 10 priests, 16 choristers, and 6 clerks, and Henry obtained a large site in the busiest part of the medieval town. It was crossed by Milne Street, from which lanes led to the High Street and to riverside wharves, and included the church of St John Zachery, Godshouse, five hostels, and many houses. All of these properties were secured and demolished, and in 1445 the Mayor and Corporation ceded all of the streets and lanes, the common land beside the river, and the quay called Salt Hythe. Common land on the west side of the river extending to Garret Hostel Lane was granted in 1447 for the recreation of the scholars. The demolition of houses and the harm caused to the river trade led to a serious loss of revenue, and in 1446 the taxes payable were reduced.

The king's enlarged plan was for a court of great splendour, the Chapel to form the north side. The east range towards the High Street would have rooms in three storeys, with a gate-tower in the centre. The two other ranges would contain a Hall, Library, lecture-rooms, and chambers, and a second smaller court was planned for a kitchen, bakehouse, brewhouse, and stables. Between the Chapel and the river there would be a cloistered cemetery, with a bell-tower 24 feet square and 120 feet high to the corbel table, and above this four turrets ending in pinnacles.

We can agree with Stow's observation: 'I suppose that if the rest of the House had proceeded according to the chapel already finished as his full intent and meaning was, the like College could scarce have been found again in any christian land.'

The first college buildings behind the Old Schools were begun in 1441, but only one range and part of a second were completed in view of the plans to build on the larger site. Actually, the Chapel was the only part of the gradiose scheme to be completed, and the old buildings continued in use until 1828. For almost 300 years, until the Fellows' Building was begun in 1724, the Chapel stood to one side of a vast expanse of grass where sheep fed.

The king laid the first stone of the Chapel in 1446, and almost 80 years were to elapse before it was finished. In spite of this long period, it retains a unity of design not found in most cathedrals having architectural designs of different periods. For the early work, a white magnesium limestone from Yorkshire, conveyed most of the way by water, was used. By 1461 the walls had risen to about 60 feet at the east end, sloping westwards to 7 to 8 feet, then little was done for about 15 years owing to the Wars of the Roses and lack of funds.

The statutes of colleges previously founded had usually given the Master only one or two rooms and an income little above that of the Fellows. The king intended that the Provost should be better lodged, and a Lodge, east of the Chapel, was ready by 1450, and existed, with alterations and additions, until 1828. Although it was the best in the university, it was said to possess only one chair, and visitors sat on stools or forms at tables supported by trestles.

Henry VI presented five great bells, estimated to weigh 10, 17, 23, 32, and 44 cwts, said to have been the first regular peal of bells and for long the largest in England. They were hung in a temporary bell-house of wood, and were frequently recast or exchanged during the next 300 years. By 1727, the three largest bells were cracked, and the college decided to sell all five to a firm in Whitechapel.

King's College was granted special privileges, including exemption from the jurisdiction of the Archbishop of Canterbury, the Bishop and the

Archdeacon of Ely, and the Chancellor of the university. The statutes of the founder placed 'at least two Fellows or scholars in each of the upper chambers, three in each of the lower chambers; each occupant is to have a separate bed; one of the Fellows is to be older than the others and is to exercise authority over his chamber-fellows and to report on their manners, conversation, and progress in their studies'.

College lectures were in existence in Godshouse, which had been removed to St Andrew's Street, in 1451, and the statutes of King's made provision for them, but the medieval system of lectures by the Regent Masters was not completely replaced by college tuition until the sixteenth century.

The practice of placing several students in each room, with one being senior to the others, helped to preserve discipline, but students who broke the rules were chastised with a rod. Dame Paston, in a letter to a tutor, encouraged him to be a stern disciplinarian: 'Prey Grenefield to send me faithfully worde ho Clemit Paston hathe do his dever i' lernyng, and if he hathe nought do welle nor wyll amende, prey him that he wyll trewly belash him tyll he wyll amende, and so did ye last maystr and ye best en he had at Caumbreg.'

The enclosure of land to form the site of King's had deprived the townspeople of lanes giving access to the river, and in 1455 Henry VI decreed that 'a certain garden called Henablay' should be granted to the town for a common passage or way to the river, from Milne Street to 'the ditch called Kinge's-diche'. The latter was not the defensive ditch, but a channel navigable for barges made in 1423 from the river near Garret Hostel Bridge, to re-enter it near the far corner of Trinity College Library, the resulting island being called Garret Hostel Green, or the Town Common.

*   *   *

The west range of the Old Schools was built between 1430 and 1460 to house the School of Canon Law. This and the earlier Divinity School were of rubble, with stone door and window frames, and externally they still retain much of their original appearance. The south range was added in 1457-70 for the Schools of Civil Law and Philosophy on the ground floor and a Library above. The quadrangle was completed by a building

on the east side which was demolished in 1754. From 1475 the Old
Schools formed a court which remained practically unchanged for 240
years.

*   *   *

Queens' College was originally founded in 1446 as the College of St
Bernard by Andrew Dockett, Rector of St Botolph's. Two years later he
gained the assistance of Queen Margaret, who asked Henry VI for
permission to refound and rename the college because 'in the whiche
Uniursite is no college founded by eny Quene of England hidertoward'.
The first small site had been on the opposite side of Milne Street, but the
First Court of the Queen's College of St Margaret and St Bernard was
commenced in 1448 on a larger site. This court was superior to any
previous college buildings, and it was quickly built.

As in many houses of the nobility constructed at this time, the gateway
gave access to a square court. It contained the Chapel, Library, Hall,
Kitchen, and chambers. Another building beside the river was erected in
about ·1460, and, later, cloisters linked this with the First Court. When
Dockett secured the patronage of Queen Elizabeth Woodville, the name
of the college became Queens'.

At this time the English archers were renowned, and a law passed in
the reign of Edward IV decreed that every Englishman must have a bow,
butts for practice must be set up in every village, and every man must
shoot up and down every feast day or be fined one halfpenny. The earliest
reference to archery in Cambridge, in 1469, describes the attitude of the
University. It was enacted that no master, scholar, servant, writer, or
stationer might carry or use a bow and arrows except for peaceful
purposes and in defence of the university privileges, after permission given
by the Chancellor.

Catharine Hall was founded in 1473 by Robert Woodlark, Provost of
King's, but none of the original buildings, forming a small court, survive.
Mainly at the expense of the university, Great St Mary's was rebuilt
between 1478 and 1519, only the thirteenth-century walls of the chancel
being retained. The roof of the nave was finished by 1508, but the tower,
begun in 1491, was not fully completed until 1608. When, by 1483, the
five easternmost bays of King's College Chapel had been completed, a
temporary wall was erected and the space covered with a timber roof.

Opposite: *King's College Chapel from the west, by David Loggan, 1688*

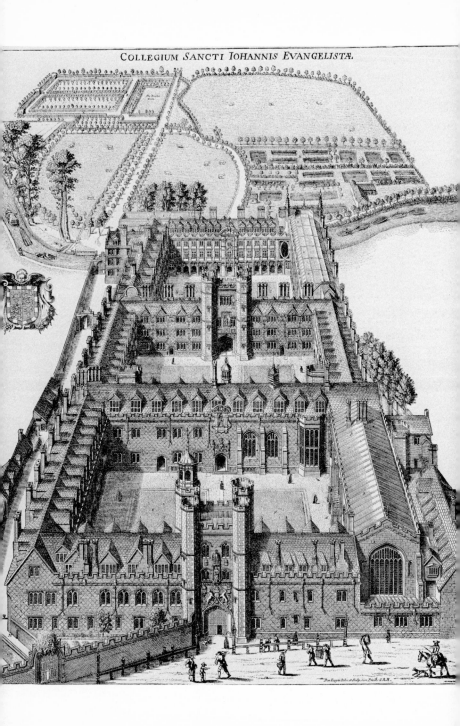

COLLEGIUM SANCTI IOHANNIS EVANGELISTÆ.

The nunnery of St Radegund had become impoverished and almost uninhabited, and in 1496 John Alcock, Bishop of Ely, obtained a licence to suppress it and to establish Jesus College for a Master, six Fellows, and a few scholars. The nuns' church was too large for this small society, so the aisles were pulled down and a wall built across the nave, one part being converted into chambers. Other parts of the nunnery, though altered, still exist.

Cranmer was a Fellow of Jesus in about 1515, but had to resign when he married the niece of the landlady of the Dolphin Inn. He was able to regain his Fellowship when his wife died in childbirth. Had she lived, he would not have become Archbishop of Canterbury.

* * *

For over 300 years the 'Town Music', sponsored by the municipality, was an important form of entertainment. The 'Waits' were originally watchmen who sounded the hours on their 'wayte-pipes' during the night. They later became an instrumental band, playing viols, hautboys, trombones, and trumpets, and took part in pageants, plays, and interludes, as well as parades to celebrate military victories, coronations, etc.

Cambridge had its own band by 1484, and the mention of waits first occurs in Borough records in 1511. They wore a livery consisting of cloaks, silver collars and chains, and a silver badge. Pepys records that 'the town musique did also come and play, but, Lord, what sad music they made! However, I was pleased with them, being all of us in very good humour.' The Town Music seems to have been disbanded in about 1790.

In the sixteenth century the town made payments to players on 57 occasions, also to minstrels, jugglers, and tumblers, the shows usually being given in private houses. William Gibbons was appointed leader of the town waits in 1567, and his famous son Orlando, the youngest of his ten children, joined the choir of King's College Chapel in 1596.

From at least 1496, the lands belonging to the colleges and the property of members of the university were exempt from clerical and lay taxes. In 1503 'privileged persons' who came under the jurisdiction of the Chancellor or Vice-Chancellor included all servants of scholars and everyone living in the households of scholars or of scholars' servants,

Opposite: *David Loggan's view of St John's College, 1688, from* **Cantabrigia Illustrata**

barbers, bookbinders, scriveners, stationers, parchment-makers, apothecaries, physicians and surgeons. In 1589 the list of privileged persons also mentioned college bakers, brewers, butchers, gardeners, the husbands of the college laundresses, the university printer and librarian, 'the man who times the university clock', and 'one plumber who shall serve the use of the university.'

Henry VII visited Cambridge in 1505 and gave 100 oaks from Chesterford Park to roof the nave of Great St Mary's. He also gave £5,000 and asked his executors to provide money to complete King's College Chapel. By 1508 over 100 men were at work, and the walls were finished by 1515. In the antechapel, the interior walls were adorned with many stone carvings with the king's crest and other symbols of the Tudor dynasty – heraldic beasts, crowns, roses, portcullises, cut in Caen stone and all different. The magnificent fan-vault, one of the supreme achievements of English architecture, was built in the next three years.

Between 1515 and 1531, when the craft of painting and firing glass had reached perfection, the large windows were glazed to form what is today the largest and best-preserved series of medieval windows in the world. During the reign of Henry VIII, the choir was paved with marble and a high altar erected, and foreign craftsmen built the organ screen, the earliest large timber structure in England completely in a Renaissance style.

The original plans had envisaged a stone screen. It was also intended that the interior stonework would be painted, the ribs of the vault in scarlet outlined in gold, and the fans blue, with gilded stars. The royal coats of arms would also have been coloured, and statues of saints would have occupied the tabernacles on the walls.

*   *   *

Early in the sixteenth century, the most influential man in the university was John Fisher, Master of Michaelhouse in 1497, Vice-Chancellor in 1501, President of Queens' in 1505, and later elected Chancellor for life. As chaplain and confessor to Lady Margaret Beaufort, mother of Henry VII, he influenced her to make important benefactions to the university. She founded the first professorship, the Lady Margaret Professorship of Divinity, and provided additional buildings and endowments for the small college of Godshouse. The name was changed to Christ's College, and she completed the First Court by providing funds for the Hall, Master's Lodge, and other buildings, to accommodate 60 scholars.

Fisher also induced Lady Margaret to convert the ancient Hospital of St John into a college, and although she died before legal provision for the project had been made, Fisher overcame all obstacles to enable the new college to open in 1516, although the First Court was not completed until 1520. St John's became the most important centre of Renaissance learning in the university.

The statutes included provisions that until after the expiration of five years from his M.A. degree, no Fellow might go into the town more often than twice a week, and whenever in the winter season a fire was lighted in the Hall, scholars and servants might stay to amuse themselves. Until the seventeenth century the students rose at the sound of the 4 a.m. bell. The great bell was rung continually from the days of the old Hospital until it was silenced during the last war.

In early times, only castles and great houses had chimneys, and college halls were heated by charcoal until comparatively modern times. Iron braziers were placed in the centre, the fumes escaping through a lantern in the roof. At Caius there was no fire in the Hall until 1564. Benefactors often gave money specifically for the provision of fires. In 1572 Dr Busby of Trinity Hall gave £20 for a common fire on Sundays at dinner and supper from 1 November until 2 February, and in 1596 W. Revell left funds for a fire of two bushels of charcoal in the Hall from November to January.

Trinity Library was not heated until 1859, and the Hall had a great wrought-iron dish, about 4 by 5 feet in diameter, standing on iron legs and filled with glowing charcoal. When this brazier was removed in 1866 it had been in use for over 160 years. There was a great shortage of fuel whenever the river was frozen and barges could not come from Lynn. The river trade in coal began in the sixteenth century, and in 1544 the Mayor and others went to Newcastle for four shiploads of coal.

It was probably John Fisher who persuaded Erasmus to come to Cambridge and reside in Queens'. Erasmus was the first teacher of Greek in the university, and during his stay he worked on his *Novum Instrumentum* and his edition of St Jerome. In letters to an Italian friend he complained about the English beer, wine, and climate, but 'The English girls are divinely pretty. Soft, pleasant, gentle, and charming . . . They have one custom which cannot be too much admired. When you go anywhere on a visit, the girls all kiss you. They kiss you when you arrive. They kiss you when you go away, and when you return.'

John Siberch, a friend of Erasmus and the first Cambridge printer, came from Cologne, and is believed to have worked in the town from 1520-1525. His press was in the King's Arms Inn, on the site of the Gate of Honour in Senate House Passage. University stationers, usually foreigners, had traded for some time, and in 1534 royal letters patent gave the university leave to appoint three stationers, printers, or booksellers to manufacture and sell approved books.

Disputes between the university and the town continued. The townsfolk were particularly incensed because the Mayor and bailiffs, on taking office, were obliged to swear an oath to maintain the privileges of the university, and officials deemed to have offended could be excommunicated. In 1529 the Mayor was excommunicated by the Vice-Chancellor, and the penalty was not lifted until he had apologised in writing and performed a penance in the church of the Austin Friars, 'holding a candle, the price of a halfpenny in his hand, and kneeling on his knees openly before the image of our Lady'. After a serious affray between the proctors and townsmen, the university renounced its right to excommunicate in temporal matters, but in 1535 and 1537 the town authorities were warned to moderate their complaints against the university.

Although the books of Martin Luther were burnt in 1520, Cambridge men who were in sympathy with his doctrines, known locally as 'the Germans', met at the White Horse Inn, which stood between the Bull and King's and acquired the nickname 'Germany'. Prominent among them were Robert Barnes, prior of the Austin Friars, and Hugh Latimer, a Fellow of Clare. Barnes, in a sermon in St Edward's in 1525, criticised the pomp of bishops and the church courts. Accused of heresy, arrested and taken to London, he had to confront Cardinal Wolsey and face a trial at Westminster. Although he finally recanted, he was not allowed to return to Cambridge. Latimer and other Cambridge men were also examined by Wolsey.

Among the many foreign Protestants who later arrived in England was

Martin Bucer from Strasburg, whose teaching in Cambridge from 1549 until his death in 1551 influenced many leading men. His funeral was attended by 3,000 persons.

To swear to the Act of Supremacy of 1534 which made the king the supreme head of the church, was to abjure the Pope. Bishop Fisher refusing to swear that oath, was executed. Thomas Cromwell became Vice-Chancellor, and the Crown began to intervene more frequently in university affairs. The Reformation and the dissolution of the monasteries caused the disappearance of the monks and friars from the university. There were fewer students, many poor scholars had to leave, and richer young men began to appear. King's College Chapel neared completion as the form of religion existing while it was being built was swept aside by the Reformation.

In 1538 the university made an unsuccessful application to the king for the conversion of religious houses into colleges. Barnwell Priory was dissolved in that year, and the others at about the same time. In 1542 the College of St Mary Magdalene replaced the monastic Buckingham College, but 50 years were to elapse before the sites of the Franciscans and the Dominicans were taken for new colleges.

The Carmelites surrendered their house to Queens', but the king divided their site between that college and King's. Dr Hatcher, Regius Professor of Physic, bought the house and grounds of the Austin Friars in 1545. A rich man, he lived in considerable style in the former Friary.

In 1545 there was a possibility that colleges might suffer the fate of the monasteries. A report about their lands and possessions was made to the king, and Archbishop Parker has described what ensued: 'The King, upon examining it, said to those of his Lords present, that he felt nowhere in his realm were so many persons maintained with so little rent, and enquired how it was that the Colleges seemed to spend more yearly than they received. We informed him that it was partly by fines for leases and from farmers for the renewal of leases and the sale of wood. Whereupon he said what a pity it would be to alter the said lands for the worse. We therefore beseeched the King that he would continue to allow us to retain our possessions such as they were. He made answer and smiled, and bade us hold our own, so we departed well armed.'

In the following year Henry VIII decided to unite the ancient colleges of King's Hall and Michaelhouse and some adjacent hostels to form

Trinity College for a Master and 60 Fellows and scholars. He granted to his new college large revenues and important privileges. Foul Lane, which crossed the present Great Court, was closed in 1551. Colleges were continually encroaching upon the common land and thoroughfares; thus in 1549 the town authorities noted: 'Item, we fynde that Trinitie College hath enclosed a common Lane, which was a common course both for cart, horse, and man, leadinge to the ryver, unto a common grene, and no recompense made therefore. Item, we fynde that Kynge's College hath taken in and enclosed Saint Austen's Lane, leadinge from the high streete unto the watersides withowte recompense. Item, we fynde that the Queens College hath taken a pece of common ground commonlye called Goslinge Grene withowte recompense.'

For Trinity College, some of the old buildings were retained, and a new Chapel was begun in 1555. In 1547 Edward VI had ordered that all shrines, tables, candlesticks, pictures, paintings and other monuments of feigned miracles, pilgrimages, idolatry and superstition, on walls or in windows, should be destroyed, and a Visitation to the university in 1549 removed all traces of the Roman Catholic religion.

Meanwhile, in 1544, a local paving act required householders to repair, and sometimes to pave, the street opposite their homes. Paving Leets were held twice-yearly in Great St Mary's, when citizens were appointed to make inspections, and offenders were fined. Many townsmen kept horses, cattle, and pigs, taking them every day to and from the common pastures, rendering 'the high stretes and lanes within the same Towne excedyngly noyed with fylth and myre lying there in great heapes'. The town fields, cultivated in small plots, extended to the boundaries of Coton, Madingley, Barton, Grantchester, Trumpington, Cherryhinton, and Ditton.

The common pastures were insufficient because aldermen had first claim on their use, and because leading burgesses had enclosed land. The poorer inhabitants claimed that the commons should be let, and the rents used to alleviate poverty. During Ket's Rebellion, a crowd demolished fences round land enclosed by a former bailiff, and threatened to do more damage. Some of the rioters were hanged, but it was agreed that henceforth the poor inhabitants could use the commons.

Statutes of 1549 altered the government of the university and the course of study. Students were forbidden card-playing, fencing, and walking about the town unaccompanied, the latter probably to avoid affrays with the townsfolk. Latimer wrote that, 'There be none now but great men's sons in Colleges and their fathers look not to have them preachers.'

Thomas Lever, in a sermon at Paul's Cross in 1550 said: 'There was in houses belonging to the university 200 students of Divinity, many well learned, which are now all clean gone, house and man, young scholars and old fatherly Doctors, not one of them left. 100 also of another sort, having rich friends or beneficed, did live by themselves in Hostels or Inns are either gone away or have crept into colleges and put poor men from bare livings ... The small number of good, diligent students now remaining only in Colleges will themselves soon have to leave unless helped.'

'There be some who rise daily between 4 and 5 in the morning, from 5 to 6 are at prayers in the chapel, from 6 to 10 private study and lectures, at 10 to dinner of a 1d piece of beef amongst 4, a small poridge of broth from the said beef with salt and oatmeal and nothing else. After this they teach or learn till 5 when supper is served not much better than dinner, then study till 9 or 10, and then, having no fires, they run up and down for half an hour to get warm before going to bed.'

In earlier times, the primary function of the university had been to train men for the church, but now more men of affairs were needed to help in government. The methods of education, too, were changing. The Regent Masters who lectured in the Schools were losing their audiences because lectures were given within the colleges. College tutors, supervising a small number of students, had a close personal relationship with them. Printing had made textbooks more accessible and diminished the need for attendance at the ordinary lectures. By the end of the sixteenth century, the college tutor had become the most important influence on a student's education.

THREE

The Sixteenth Century, 1550–1590

On the death of Edward VI in 1553, the Council proclaimed Lady Jane Grey queen, and took steps to arrest the Lady Mary, who stayed near Cambridge at Sawston Hall. The Duke of Northumberland, who supported Lady Jane Grey, arrived with an army of 8,000 foot and 2,000 horse, but his men deserted him, and Mary was proclaimed queen in London. Northumberland, attempting to save himself, proclaimed Mary in front of the market cross, but was arrested in King's, taken to London, and executed.

On the accession of Mary and her marriage to Philip of Spain, all the acts of her predecessor affecting religion were repealed, the church was reunited with Rome and mass was again celebrated. Latimer, Ridley, and Cranmer, bishops who had been educated at Cambridge, were burned alive at Oxford, and John Hullier suffered a similar fate on Jesus Green.

All of the college Masters except three and many Fellows were removed; at St John's 14 Fellows went into exile. During the reign of Mary, only those who subscribed to the Roman Catholic religion could obtain a degree. In 1556 Archbishop Parker instructed that surplices must be worn in church. Leading Protestants objected, and at St John's most of the members attended without surplices. The Master was forced to promise that he would ensure that the instruction was obeyed.

A Commission was appointed to inspect the university and to see that the old form of religion had been completely re-established. The members arrived in Cambridge in January 1557, and forbade the celebration of divine service in Great St Mary's and St Michael's because the eminent German Protestants, Martin Bucer and Paul Fagius, had been buried in these churches.

The corpses were exhumed, the coffins bound to a stake on Market Hill, and then burned, together with heretical books. On the following day, the Bishop of Chester hallowed a large tub of water, adding salt, ashes, and wine, and walked three times outside and three times inside Great St Mary's to reconcile the building. On the next day, there was a great procession, and St Michael's was similarly hallowed.

John Caius refounded Gonville Hall in 1557. He had entered as a student in 1529, then studied medicine under Versalius in Padua, became a professor, then physician to Edward VI and Mary. By middle life he could have retired to a fine country seat, but when he was 48 he handed over many of his possessions to his old college, and returned to a demanding life at St Bartholomew's Hospital. In 1557 the Fellows of Gonville Hall begged him to become their Master, and when he acquiesced he found that neglect and bad administration had brought the college to the verge of ruin.

In Italy and France he had become familiar with Renaissance architecture, and for Gonville Hall he designed noble new buildings. His Second Court had only three sides 'lest the air, from being confined within a narrow space, should become foul'. He decreed that anyone who should throw dirt or offal into the court would be fined.

He combined with these practical considerations a love of symbolism. He designed three gates; a student entered the college through the modest Gate of Humility; during his residence he would often pass through the Gate of Virtue erected in 1567 and one of the earliest buildings in the country in a pure Renaissance style. Finally, the student would go through the Gate of Honour to take his degree.

Caius is a tragic figure because although he did so much for the college, giving it estates, books, and plate, he had constant difficulties with the Fellows. Most of them were young and bitter Puritans, whereas his sympathies were with the older faith. After he had been Master for 14 years, the Fellows, encouraged by the Vice-Chancellor and the Master of Trinity, raided his rooms and found symbols of Catholicism which they burnt. The Vice-Chancellor, in a letter to Lord Burghley, said that this had been done 'with the willing hartes of ye whole Company of that house'.

Caius retired to St Bartholomew's, but returned near the end of his life on a litter to make arrangements for the construction of his tomb under the altar of the Virgin Mary. When he died in London, his body was brought to Cambridge, when 'all degrees in the University met him in honourable manner near Trumpington Ford and conducted him with the greatest funeral pomp to the college where he was buried in the Chapel'. When the Chapel was rebuilt, his monument was placed on a wall. 'His Body was found whole and perfect, and the Beard very long, though it had been buried there near 150 Years.'

John Caius was mainly responsible for the introduction of the practical study of anatomy in England, and he obtained from Queen Elizabeth the right to have the bodies of two criminals or unknown strangers each year for dissection in Gonville and Caius College.

Most colleges have no records of their early students, and Caius is almost unique in having lists of pensioners for a number of years early in the sixteenth century. Dr Caius began a proper register in 1560. The largest group were monks, next came parochial clergy who obtained leave from their bishop to study at Cambridge for two to three years. There were a few rich and well-connected priests, and a few men whose parents were well-to-do or who belonged to the professional classes.

Students were divided into those supported by the foundation, pensioners who paid for their board and lodging, and sizars, poor men who were boarded, lodged and educated free, and in return acted as servants to the Master, Fellows, and Fellow-Commoners. Many sizars had distinguished careers, becoming Fellows and Tutors, and at Caius, four out of eight of the Masters after Caius had entered as sizars.

Many men remained in college throughout the year, even during the Long Vacation. Roads were bad, and those with homes at a distance remained in college for Christmas owing to the difficulty and danger of undertaking long journeys in the winter. During the Christmas period, masks, revels, and games were permitted in the Hall. Students rose at 6, dinner was at 10, supper at 6, and Dr Caius ordered that students must go to bed at 8.

In medieval times, the maintenance of the public highways was a manorial obligation. From 1555 until 1835 it was, with some exceptions, a public duty. Each parish was required annually to appoint unpaid surveys to organize those local persons who were obliged to help to repair the roads.

Students could not claim exemption. In 1570 the Vice-Chancellor decreed 'that no inhabitant within the town of Cambridge, being either scholar or scholar's servant, can or may be privileged by that title from the common day's work of mending the highways, but that all and singular shall either work or find sufficient labourer, upon the pain limited in the statute.' In the seventeenth century, increased traffic rendered this method inadequate, and parochial authorities were empowered to levy highway rates, though at first few did so. Parishes failing to maintain their roads were sometimes summoned under common law for permitting a nuisance.

Many roads were constructed or maintained from funds given by citizens. In 1558 Dr Henry Harvey of Trinity Hall paid for a causeway to be made from Cambridge to Quy. Fuller, in his *Worthies,* states that it was constructed 'for the convenience of passengers in those dirty ways, so that his bounty hath made summer for them in the depth of winter'. Carter says that, 'in mentioning this Cause-way, I can't forbear taking notice of a Jest, a certain Nobleman put upon the Dr. one Morning, as he was overlooking the Workmen ... "Dr," says he, "I imagine you think this Cause-way is the Highway to Heaven." To whom the other replied, "No, no, Sir; for then I should not have met you in this Place." '

In 1563, Thomas Johnson, citizen and haberdasher of London, gave 13s 4d for the highways between Barkway and Dogshead in the Pot, otherwise called Horemayd, and 26s 8d for the highway between Trumpington and Hauxton Mill. Dr Mowse of Trinity Hall, in his will dated 30 May 1586, left money for repairs to roads. Robert Hare added to this bequest the income from an estate to be applied to mend the highway between Cambridge and Barkway. A German visitor in 1592 stated that the road between London and Cambridge travelled through villainous, boggy, and wild country, very little inhabited. In 1615 Dr Perse gave £10 per annum for repairing the causeway from the end of Jesus Lane to Quy Causeway.

* * *

On the accession of Queen Elizabeth in 1558, many Masters were dismissed and the work of the Reformation was resumed. The university received new statutes, giving increased powers to the Vice-Chancellor and Masters, and these remained in force until the middle of the nineteenth century. Students were forbidden to play dice and, except at Christmas, cards; daily resorting to taverns; vain clubbing of money; sword-playing, fencing, and dancing-schools; gaming houses; cock-fighting, bear or bull baiting; quoits; or looking on at any of these. The privileges of the university were again increased by a royal charter of 1561.

The Puritans wished to eliminate music from church services, and early in Elizabeth's reign a proposal to ban organs in all churches was only narrowly rejected. The churchwardens of Great St Mary's sold the organ case in 1613 and had presumably also taken down the organ. When the use of Latin for public prayers was abolished, the universities obtained exemption, but soon after abandoned the use of Latin in services.

In 1557 the use of stone-bows (i. e. catapults) was forbidden: 'as great destruction had been caused to dovehouses and the glass of churches, chapels, and college halls. And because pewter vessels were melted down to supply pellets'. Many colleges had dove-cots; the dovehouse of Peterhouse was repaired in 1546, and in 1573 it was leased for 21 years to William Cooke for 40s a year, he to leave it with at least six dozen old pigeons. In 1577 a contract was made with John Cooper of Steeple Bumpstead in Essex, carpenter, whereby in consideration of the erection of a dovecot within the college precincts, the worthy craftsman's son, Thoma Cooper, a Scholar of Ely, was to be awarded a Bible Clerkship 12d per week, with chambers, commons, and other allowances, for seven years.

In 1560 the university ordained that 'No scholler doe weare any long lockes of Hayre uppon his heade, but that he be polled, notted, or rounded.' Shirts to be plain and not mixed with silk. Hose not to be silk, and 'blacke or sad-colour neere unto blacke, excepte white Hose for boys' Gowns to be made of cloth and in the fashion of the Priest's gown, and coloured black or russet. Cloaks also to be made only of cloth 'of blacke or sad-colour'. Hats, no colour but black.

In the same year it was decreed that the inhabitants must pay rates so that ladders and fire-hooks could be provided to combat fires, and that the university for its part should pay for leather buckets. The ladders and buckets were kept in various locations, and the fire-hooks in the churches of Great St Mary's, St Botolph, and St Sepulchre. The hooks, fixed to the end of long poles, were used to tear off the thatched roof of a burning house. One of these fire-hooks may still be seen in St Bene't's.

*   *   *

Queen Elizabeth spent five days in Cambridge in 1564, and in anticipation of her coming the Vice-Chancellor and Masters were 'advertised to put themselves in readiness to pleasure her Majestie and to welcome her with all manner of scholastic exhibitions, viz., with sermons both in English and in Latin, disputations in all kinds of faculties, and the playing of comedies and tragedies, orations and verses, both in Latin and Greek, to be made and set up by all students in the way that her Majestie should go or ride'.

'Beer, ale and wine was sent to King's and divers officers of the Court repaired to the town to take up the Queen's lodging and to know when any dyed of the plague.' The Vice-Chancellor and the Mayor ensured that the town was well paved and that every inhabitant provided sufficient sand to cover the streets. The Corporation mace was regilded, and market cross repaired, the gallows mended. Scholars were instructed to kneel lowly and cry 'Vivat Regina' as the Queen passed.

Elizabeth rode from Haslingfield, where she had spent the night, and 'The Mayor of the Town . . . met her Majestie a little above Newnham, on horseback . . . and so came to Newnham Mills . . . And there . . . she alighted and went into the miller's yard and house for a little space.' Then she continued on her way, 'dressed in a gown of black velvet pinked and a hat that was spangled with gold, and a bush of feathers'.

Opposite Queens', a large gate had been placed across the street to keep out the crowds, and between the college and the west end of King's College Chapel the way was lined with scholars. When the procession reached King's, the town officials had to leave, as they had 'no authority or jurisdiction in that place'. At the Chapel, everyone alighted except the Queen, and the Provost and Fellows made a lane on the way to the choir, through the Chapel decorated with tapestries and rich crimson velvets.

The Public Orator, kneeling, made a speech praising the Queen, during which she often shook her head and bit her lips, saying 'Non est veritas,' but when he praised her virginity, she commended him, and congratulated him because he had spoken without pause or hesitation for half an hour.

She attended evensong, and on the following day, a Sunday, Dr Perne preached a sermon in Latin. In the evening she heard prayers, then a comedy lasting until midnight was acted in the Chapel. A great stage had been erected in Great St Mary's for plays and disputations, and during the remainder of her visit she went to other colleges, listened and sometimes replied to numerous speeches in Greek or Latin, and 'If the Queen were weary at the Comedies (as no doubt she was, they being meanly performed), she dissembled her uneasiness very artfully'.

It is also recorded that 'At her entrance all men were upon the knee, nor did any one presume to rise until leave was given ... The greatest peer, the Duke of Norfolk, and the greatest favourite, Robert Dudley, addressed her majesty upon the knee.' Oxford sent its Proctors and the chief Bedell 'to see and hear, as near as they could, for their better instructions (if it should fortune the Queen's Majestie to visit that Universitie) all our doings, order and proceedings'.

She was so well pleased that she remained in Cambridge for an extra day, and would have stayed longer if provision of beer and ale could have been made. She objected to the wives of Masters being in college, and Baker says that this rule was 'generally observed till towards the times of the usurpation, when all things run into confusion and wives and their dependancies were brought in to the disturbance of scholars'.

A new code of statutes of 1570 gave complete control of university affairs to the Vice-Chancellor and the Heads of Houses, the powers of the Caput were increased, and those of the Proctors diminished.

Until 1574 the only direct approach to the Schools was by the narrow East Schools Street, but at the expense of Archbishop Parker a new street called Regent Walk or University Street was constructed from opposite the west door of Great St Mary's. In the last quarter of the century, colleges built or improvised accommodation for the increased number of students who paid for their board and lodging.

The great hall and chamber of the castle had already become ruinous when Henry VI had allowed King's to cart away stone for their buildings. By the reign of Elizabeth, only the large gateway and a section of the curtain wall remained.

The river towards Grantchester was dangerous, choked with weeds and had many deep holes, and this may have prompted the Masters to issue a decree 'That no one goe into the water.' Penalties for disobedience were severe; for a first offence a scholar could be sharply and severely scourged openly and publicly in his college hall, and similarly chastised in the Schools on the following day. For a second offence he could be expelled.

The university often complained about the diversions of the townsmen, saying on one occasion that they 'endevord by theire bearbaytinge and bullbaytings, and such like vaine games, to hinder the quiet of the Universitie, and to draw over the students from their bookes.'

A number of wealthy men built country seats in the county and began to interest themselves in the affairs of the town. Lord North, who had a mansion and a large estate at Kirtling, became Lord Lieutenant in 1569 and High Steward of the Borough in 1572. He championed the town in conflicts with the university, and the Council gave him many silver-gilt cups and other presents to express their gratitude. From 1572 the Orders of the Town Council, hitherto in Latin, were written in English. For a long time, many books continued to be published in Latin, e.g. Newton's *Principia,* a mathematical book on astronomy, in 1687.

In 1556, the Town Council had ordered that all of the townsfolk must attend the sermon in their parish church or in Great St Mary's; offenders had to pay a fine. Since the Reformation, sermons had become of increased importance. There were no newspapers or magazines, and the pulpit was almost the only way in which new ideas could be presented to the public.

Until late Victorian days, the Sunday University Sermon in Great St Mary's was a great event, attended by most of the university and many townsfolk. Cranmer, Latimer, and Ridley had preached there, and the church can claim to have a closer connection with the birth of the Reformation than any other. Men liked to listen to sermons; Archbishop Tillotson, in his student days, heard four sermons in different churches on Sundays. After Dr Chadderton, the first Master of Emmanuel, had once preached for two hours, he was urged to continue and did so for another hour.

The sermons were often controversial, dealing with religious beliefs or practices, or matters affecting the university. Thomas Cartwright, a Fellow of Trinity and appointed Lady Margaret Professor of Divinity in 1569, was a strong Puritan and a very eloquent preacher who expressed his views so vehemently that he came into conflict with his Master, John

Whitgift, and was expelled from his offices. For the next 30 years he was the leader of the English Puritans.

*   *   *

During the reign of Elizabeth, the number of students increased considerably, from about 1,200 in 1564 to about 1,800 in 1573. By the end of the reign there were nearly 2,000. Caius calculated that in 1574 between one half and one third were pensioners. Elizabeth's statutes forbade the admission of boys under 14, and gradually the average age of entry rose, though there were still some very young freshmen. In 1578 four brothers named Grimston, aged 14, 15, 16, and 18 were admitted at the same time to Caius. Nicolas Ferrar came up in 1606 when only 13, Jeremy Taylor entered Caius in 1626 at the same age, and Pitt entered Pembroke in 1773 at 14.

Offending students were often severely punished. A letter of 1569 from Lord North to the Vice-Chancellor regarding a student who had spoken 'evyll and fowle words' to the Mayor, ordered that as he was a student 'he shall but onley stand upon the Pillorye and have one of his eares nayled to the same by the space of three howrs.' He added that had the offender been a townsman, 'he should have lost both hys eares.'

Townswomen convicted of being common scolds were placed in the ducking chair which hung by a pulley fastened to a beam near the middle of the Great Bridge, and were immersed three times in the water.

As an example of the powers of the Vice-Chancellor to punish townsmen, there is the case of Thos P. and Emma B. who, in 1571, were accused of adultery. He decreed 'That they shall be tied at a cart's tail, with the upper parts of their bodies naked, and be whipped in manner and form following: That is to say, first to be carried from Magdalene College until the farther end of the bridge, and there, after proclamation made, to receive three stripes apiece with a rod. This to be repeated at six places in various parts of the town, after which they are to be handed over to the constable with their passports and sent out of the town.'

Regulations to restrict entertainments that might cause students to neglect their work, also curtailed the pleasures of the townsfolk. Plays in Latin were performed in the colleges, but professional players coming to

Cambridge were liable to be imprisoned as vagabonds. In 1574 the university prohibited 'showes of unlawful, hurtfull, and pernicious and unhonest games' (probably plays), within five miles of the town.

In 1580 the county magistrates granted a licence for games to be held at Howes on the Huntingdon Road, but following objections from the university the licence was revoked, and in 1583 the Vice-Chancellor bribed actors to keep away from Cambridge. In 1590 we learn that the tragedy *Roxana* was acted in the Hall of Trinity with such life-like passion that a gentlewoman 'fell distracted and never after recovered her senses.'

Bull and bear-baiting were prohibited for four to five miles round the town. In 1581 Dr Perne complained to Lord Burleigh about bear-baiting at Chesterton on a Sunday, when the Proctor, Bedell, and several M.A.s found a great multitude of young scholars. 'He there found the beare at stake, where he had been bayted in the sermon time, between one and two o'clock in the afternoon. He asked the bearward by what authoritie he bayted his beare there, who answered that he was Lord Vaux's man and had a warrant from the justices.' The Proctor replied that it contravened the privileges of the university, and 'commanded the bearward to cease from that disordered pastime, to which the bearward submitted'. The crowd abused the Proctor, and 'violently shoved and thrust the Bedell upon the beare, in sort that he cold hardly keepe himself from hurt'.

In 1575 the university and the town made regulations to cleanse and light the streets, prevent nuisances, and combat pestilence and fire. After complaining about persons who 'not only suffer their cannels and streets to lye uncleansed, but also lay their muck, mire, dung, filth, and other annoyance in the high streets,' they ordered that the streets should be cleaned and swept twice a week, and carters were to be appointed to carry the muck to the common dunghills. Innkeepers or others who kept more than four horses or bullocks must only deposit muck or dung in the highways when the carters were about to call.

The Vice-Chancellor and the Mayor would annually appoint two men in each parish to see that the streets were cleaned, and two burgesses and two scholars in every ward were to assess the contributions to be made by the inhabitants towards the wages of the carters. Butchers might slay beasts only in the common slaughterhouses. Pigs must not be allowed in the streets 'without a driver,' and ducks and geese must not be allowed to roam the streets.

There were regulations 'for better provision against the casualty of fire'. A specified number of buckets, scoops, and ladders were to be kept in each college, and others, also fire-hooks, in four churches. In the event of a fire, two university Proctors and two constables should repair there at once and enlist suitable scholars and townsmen to labour to quench the fire.

There were provisions for the seclusion of the afflicted in times of plague, and for the destruction of their possessions. People who left a house where there were infected persons could be fined for the first two offences, but a third default would entail perpetual banishment from the town.

Lanterns and candle lights were to placed in the evenings in places named by the authorities, from the feast of All Saints until the feast of the Purification of the Virgin Mary, 'except such nights as the moon shall shine.' Early in the seventeenth century, watchmen called upon people to show their candle or lantern lights. Wages for the crier appear in the Treasurer's accounts for 1615: 'Item, to a fellowe that cried candell light for xij weeks, xij,' and in 1616: 'Item, to him that crieth lanthorne and candell light, xij.' Similar charges appear annually until 1672.

*   *   *

Upon the dissolution of the monasteries, the king had given the buildings of the Franciscans to Trinity, and some were partially demolished to provide stone for extensions to the college. The house of the Dominicans, after belonging to several different persons, was purchased in 1583 by Sir Walter Mildmay, Chancellor of the Exchequer to Queen Elizabeth, to form the site of Emmanuel College.

The former monastic buildings were adapted, the chapel being converted into a Hall, and the refectory into a Chapel. On the St Andrew's Street frontage a long range with short wings was built, and another building to the south side of Front Court. Sir Walter intended his college to prepare men for the Church, and early in the seventeenth century it became the principal centre for Puritanism. For a time it had more undergraduates than Trinity or St John's. Christ's and Emmanuel were the most Puritan colleges, training men to preach in a manner that could be understood by the common people.

Rules of the University Library of 1582 included provisions 'that none tarry at one booke above one hour' and 'Before the keeper goe out of the Librarie, he shall view all the Bookes, and if any be left open or out of their due place, he shall safely close them up, and set them in their places.' In 1586 a Grace prohibited booksellers from buying books printed in London which had been, or should be, printed in Oxford or Cambridge.

At Peterhouse, a Library was built in 1590, when Dr Andrew Perne, Master and five times Vice-Chancellor, bequeathed his books and money. He alone among the high authorities of the university had retained his posts throughout the Reformation period. Under Edward VI he was a staunch Protestant, an ardent Catholic under Mary, when the bodies of the Protestant foreigners Bucer and Fagius were exhumed and burned, and a Protestant again in the reign of Elizabeth. Contemporaries invented the Latin verb *pernare,* meaning to be a turncoat, to change often.

At Peterhouse he erected a weathervane with the initials A.P. which his critics said stood for A Protestant, A Papist, or A Puritan. When this was blown down in a storm, it was acquired by the Rev. Cole, the well-known antiquary, who erected it on his barn. Twelve years later, in 1782, when the steeple of St Peter's in Castle Street was being repaired, he arranged for it to be placed there, and this attractive piece of metalwork remains there to this day.

FOUR

The Seventeenth Century, 1590-1640

Hamond's Plan of 1592, measuring nearly 4 feet x 3 feet, shows in remarkable detail the streets and buildings at that time. A traveller approaching from London came upon the first buildings at Spital End, or the corner of Lensfield Road. To the left was pasture, then houses from the present site of the Fitzwilliam Museum to Peterhouse. Buildings on the street frontage obscured the three-sided court closed on the eastern side by a wall, and the main entrance was in the north range through the churchyard of Little St Mary's. Opposite was the single small court of Pembroke.

Between Mill Lane and Silver Street were many houses and the Cardinal's Cap Inn. Five inns and many houses were on the left, and the Dolphin Inn and houses where is now the New Court of Corpus. The High Street (King's Parade) was exceedingly narrow, with shops and houses on both sides. In front of King's, they covered all the space between the present Screen and the kerb, and a wall surrounded the large and still vacant site secured by Henry VI, the college consisting only of the Chapel and the small court behind the Schools.

University Street was walled on both sides near the Schools, and houses and the New Inn stood on the site of the Senate House. In Trinity Street, buildings still obscured Caius. From the small Gate of Humility a walled passage led to the Gate of Virtue, and there were entrances to the two small courts in Findsilver Lane (Trinity Lane).

The tower of Great St Mary's was not completed until 1608; there was a house on each side of the west door and more against the eastern and part of the northern walls. On the site now occupied by Bowes &

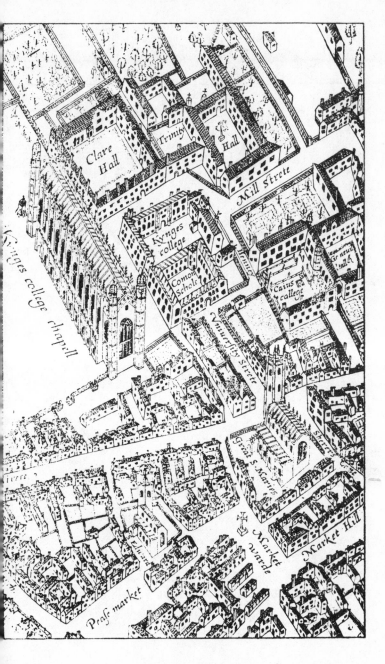

Bowes was a large house, already a bookshop in 1581. Early in the seventeenth century William Scarlett was there, and an unbroken line of booksellers have continued until today. It is not only the oldest bookshop in the country, but the site where the same retail trade has been carried on for the longest time.

A walled passage led to the Great Gate of Trinity; a range of chambers projected into the court from a point south of the Gate, and from the west side another range extended halfway towards the Gate.

Beyond the First Court of St John's was a small quadrangle which was removed when the Second Court was built. St John's Street was narrow until it was widened on both sides in the nineteenth century, and the tower of All Saints projected over the footway. Beyond St John's, a lane leading to a riverside quay was not closed until 1863, and numerous houses bordered Bridge Street, with others in courts and alleys behind.

Turning to the right, the upper part of the Round Church was polygonal with battlements until altered in 1841. On the left was the Hoop Inn, with the Dolphin opposite on the present site of Whewell's Court. Christ's had a single court, and beside St Andrew's Church was the Brazen George, acquired by the college c.1636 to accommodate pensioners. The Blackfriar's site had become Emmanuel College in 1584, and Christ's Pieces was still arable land.

There were a great many inns and most of them were large. The town was a convenient stopping-place on the way north, or for people travelling between East Anglia and the Midlands, and Sturbridge Fair attracted buyers and merchants from afar. The inns usually had a narrow street frontage, with a large gateway giving access to a yard, the exit being in another street because coaches and waggons could not turn in the yard. On both sides were open galleries from which the rooms were entered.

One of the leading inns was the Rose, its courtyard now Rose Crescent. For many years it was kept by the Wolf family; many students lodged there, and it became known as Wolf's College. When Michael Wolf died in 1618, it had 42 rooms, excluding garrets. Most of the bedrooms had carpets, wall-hangings, and bed-curtains, and Wolf owned 300 ounces of gold and silver plate. Pepys stayed several times at the Rose; on one occasion he 'lay very ill, by reason of some drunken scholars making a noise all night'. Much Council business was transacted here, and although the east part at the corner of Rose Crescent has been rebuilt, there still exists the balcony from which parliamentary candidates addressed the townsfolk.

In Market Street, the Angel, with a yard to Green Street, was almost as important as the Rose. The yard of the Black Bear, the inn in which Cromwell's officers met during the Civil War, is now Market Passage, and opposite was the Crane. In Petty Cury, the Falcon, with a frontage of 50 feet, was the principal inn in the town. Until comparatively recent times, the fifteenth- and sixteenth-century buildings of three storeys on both sides of the yard had open galleries which accommodated the quality when plays were being performed below. Queen Mary and Queen Elizabeth both saw plays there.

At the Red Lion, recently demolished, the courtyard had been covered over, but waiters still had to cross it to carry food from the kitchen to the dining-room. In Peas Hill was another tavern frequented by Pepys: 'To the Three Tuns, where we drank pretty hard and many healths to the King'. At the east end of Petty Cury stood the Wrestlers, a most picturesque early seventeenth-century building, with oriels and gables at the rear.

In Bene't Street, the Eagle and Child still survives; many coaches once left from it, and at one time it was also the Post Office. Opposite, in 1592, the church and the former site of the Austin Friars were surrounded by walls, and the entrance to the Old Court of Corpus was through the churchyard until 1500, when the parish ceded a strip of ground for a passage. Among all of the early college courts, that of Corpus is least changed, although the present Hall replaced the old kitchen and library in 1823. South of Old Court was the Master's Gallery and the Chapel of 1579-84, both destroyed to make room for New Court.

The Market Place, the heart of the medieval town, contained the Guildhall, prison, fountain, cross, stocks, and pillory, and many of the principal inns overlooked it or were in adjoining streets. Until 1849 it was an L-shaped area occupying the east and south sides of the present Square. A rectangular block of shops and houses covered the north-west part, the very narrow Pump Lane or Warwick Street dividing them from houses built against the wall of Great St Mary's.

Corn, poultry, and butter were sold on the north side of the market, vegetables in the centre, milk west of the market cross, and meat in shambles on the south side, in front of the Guildhall. An ordinance of 1579 had provided that 'all fresh-water and sea fish brought to the town and all the common fishmongers which usually have stood in the market over against the new shambles shall from henceforth be sold on the Pease Market Hill and have their standing there'. The fish market remained in Peas Hill until 1949. A block of houses adjoined the east end of St Edward's; the last of these was not removed until 1874.

Lyne's map of 1574 shows the Cross raised on stone steps and protected by a lead-covered roof destroyed in 1587. It was rebuilt in 1664, but disappeared in 1786 when the Council appointed a committee to choose a new site 'if they shall think a Cross necessary'. As it is not mentioned again, the committee apparently decided not to erect it elsewhere.

Hamond's Plan shows many pumps, some sited in churchyards. The parish pump of St Giles stood at the corner of Chesterton Lane, beside the churchyard wall. When a grave was re-opened, it was found to be half full of water, and while attempting to bale out this water, the gravedigger decided to try the pump. The water in the grave drained away, and the hole through which it was escaping was located and sealed, but henceforth this pump ceased to be used for drinking-water.

There are 'Pump Courts' in Queens' and Jesus. At Caius, there was a pump from which the bedmakers drew water for washing and drinking, although on the opposite side of the wall was a privy. There was another pump in Gonville Court and a third near the kitchen. The college accounts record frequent payments for repairs, and a pump mender was employed at regular wages.

Hamond's Plan shows many areas thickly covered with domestic buildings which have since been demolished to make way for college and commercial developments. As the population increased, the extent of the built-up area remained almost unchanged. Existing houses were divided into small tenements, and in 1597 the Privy Council wrote to the town authorities about 'certain inhabitants seeking their private gain with hurtful results to the whole University and Town. Not only do they erect houses on spare ground, they also subdivide the houses into parts, and let them to the poorest persons, whereby the University and Town are overburdened in maintaining the poor'. An enquiry was set up to establish how many such houses had been built or divided in the preceding ten years, and measures were taken to remove inhabitants where numbers were excessive.

In 1593, when London theatres were closed because of the plague, the Vice-Chancellor complained to the Queen about wandering players in Cambridge, and prayed 'to be freed from players, that badd kind of people who are, as wee thinke, the most ordinary carriers and dispensers of the infection of the plague'. On 6 September 1594, flood water carried away the Great Bridge and those of King's and St John's.

James I, in 1604, forbade 'Bear-baiting, bull-baiting, common plaies, public shewes, enterludes, comoedies or tragedies in the English language, and games at loggats and nine-holes.' Loggats resembled the game of skittles, and nine-holes was similar to bagatelle. In 1606 there was a serious riot during a play performed in King's Hall, when it was said that divers Noblemen, Doctors, etc., had been put in imminent danger of their lives.

In 1594 the executors of Frances Sidney, Countess of Sussex, obtained the site of the Franciscans for a college of a Master, 10 Fellows, and 20 Scholars. The refectory was divided into two floors, the lower for the Chapel, the upper for the Library, and Ralph Symons erected two ranges of buildings on the north and south sides, with a Hall and Lodge on the east.

In St John's, in 1598, 70 men lived in 28 rooms, and the college built a Second Court in 1598-1602 at the expense of the Countess of Shrewsbury. Baker's History of the college records that 'It was Mr. Bois' observation that about this time, as the college began to rise in buildings, so it declined in learning; which was certainly very true, for the master not long after his coming hither having brought them the agreeable news of a new court, they were so overjoyed or so overbusied with architecture, that their other studies were intermitted and the noise of axes and hammers disturbed them in their proper business.' This court is a fine example of Tudor brick architecture.

Dr Thomas Nevile, a rich man and a favourite of Queen Elizabeth, was appointed Master of Trinity in 1593. Between 1597 and 1605 he had some of the existing buildings demolished, and erected others to form the largest court in either Oxford or Cambridge. King Edward's Tower, erected in 1428-32 as the entrance to King's Hall, was taken down and re-erected in line with the Chapel, The statue of Edward III depicts him holding a sword impaling the three crowns of England, France, and Scotland, and below is his motto, *Fama super aethera notus,* known by fame beyond the skies.

The Hall, the largest in Cambridge, and the beautiful octagonal fountain, the only large ornamental fountain of its period still in existence, were built at Nevile's expense. He next built a Second Court, completed in 1614, although it then extended to just over half of its present size, being closed by a wall with a gate in the centre. Trinity men became Archbishop of Canterbury and of York, seven others bishops, eleven deans, and ten professors, during Nevile's mastership.

By the end of the sixteenth century the hostels had disappeared and many colleges had put up new buildings. College tutors had replaced lectures given by the Regent Masters, each of them supervising only a few students, while the Regius Professors gave more advanced teaching. Nobles and rich men were sending their sons to be trained as men of affairs. Plays and other entertainments were again prohibited by a charter of 1605, and university officials were empowered to search for prostitutes and for scholars wandering about by night.

*   *   *

The ravages of the Great Plague towards the end of the sixteenth century caused people to be concerned about the filthy state of the King's Ditch and to consider a better water supply. Matthew Parker, in a book published in 1574, wrote that he earnestly wished that the little new river near Vandlebury might be brought to the City of Cambridge by Trumpington Ford, to wash the King's Ditch, and foretold that then 'no City would be finer than Cambridge, and the memory of so great an Action would not be so grateful to Posterity as pleasing to the Inhabitants'.

Attached to a history of Cambridge by him was a plan by Lyne dated 1574 on which there is a marginal note in Latin that 'the King's Ditch ... now serves ... for carrying off the sewage and for washing away ordure into the River Granta. But if Cambridge people would subscribe of their resources, and would arrange so that the stream which there is at the ford of Trumpington should flush out the Ditch, there would be no town pleasanter than Cambridge'. Dr Perne, in a letter to Lord Burghley, made similar suggestions.

In 1610 the scheme was carried out. From Vicar's Brook, near Long Road, an artificial channel called the Little New River was made to the conduit head at the corner of Lensfield Road. From here the water was distributed by three routes; the first, down Trumpington Street to meet the King's Ditch at Mill Lane. In 1614 a supply of water was conveyed through lead pipes via Tennis Court Road, St Andrew's Hill, and Guildhall Place to a conduit on the Market Hill. A third open channel made in 1631 led water along Lensfield Road and then turned northwards to feed ponds and a bathing-pool in Emmanuel and a bathing-pool in Christ's.

At various points where the water was piped, there were dipping-holes from which the inhabitants could fill their buckets, and the Little New River was a main source of drinking-water for 250 years. It is doubtful whether the original aim of scouring the King's Ditch was achieved, as the volume of water was probably insufficient and it flowed too sluggishly.

The conduit which was built in the market and later removed to the corner of Lensfield Road is commonly called 'Hobson's Conduit,' although he was only one of a number of persons who planned and carried out the scheme. Born in 1544, he was for 60 years a leading figure in the town. From 1570 until 1630 his large 6- and 8-horse waggons made a weekly journey from The George, an inn owned by him which was in Trumpington Street, to The Bull in Bishopsgate Street, London. The roads were so bad that each trip took three days or more. He carried letters and goods, and sometimes passengers.

He kept 40 horses for hire, and the phrase 'Hobson's choice, that or none,' arose because he always insisted that the animal that had been rested for the longest time should be taken. He became one of the wealthiest citizens, known to all the Heads and Fellows of the colleges, the students and townsfolk. He founded a charitable trust to build a Spinning House on the site of the old Police Station in St Andrew's Street, to provide work for the unemployed and to serve as a house of correction for rogues and vagabonds. For one of his daughters he purchased Anglesey Abbey, lately the home of Lord Fairhaven, and her descendants lived there for over a century.

Milton, in his *Pleasant Conceits,* 1607, records an occasion when Hobson gave a great banquet. 'The guests, expecting a great cheare, they were all disappoynted: for what found they, thinke you? Nothing, on my word, but each one a cup of wine and a manchet of bread on a trencher, and some five hundred candles lighted about the room, which was a very light banquet, both for the inner man and for the eye.' Until his 86th year he drove a waggon, but in 1630 the plague was so bad in Cambridge that colleges were closed, and communications with London forbidden. The enforced idleness caused him to sicken and take to his bed, and within a few months he had died.

In 1616 the university complained that the town authorities were 'pestering every Lane and Corner with unholsome Cottages,' and in 1632 said that in one street, 151 persons were living in 26 houses.

Only some of the clergy were licensed to preach; the majority could only read the prescribed service. A type of service known as a Lecture, consisting mainly of a sermon, was popular, and the Borough had a public preacher by 1610. These were men of academic distinction, and were appointed by the Mayor. A number of puritan clergymen preached at Holy Trinity, and galleries had to be built to accommodate the crowds. These 'Town Sermons,' were very popular, and they continued until about 1750.

From 1610 until 1640 there were more students than at any time during the next 200 years, and several colleges were enlarged. Education was still medieval in character, but there were reformers like Francis Bacon who disapproved of the emphasis on the philosophy of Aristotle. In his *Advancement of Learning* (1605), he condemned the chief subject taught as 'vain matter. This kind of degenerate learning did chiefly reign amongst the schoolmen; who having sharp and strong wits, and abundance of leisure, and small variety of reading; but their wits being shut up in the cells of a few authors (chiefly Aristotle their dictator), as their persons were shut up in the cells of monasteries and colleges; and knowing little of history, either of nature or time; did out of no great quantity of matter and infinite agitation of wit, spin out unto us those laborious webs of learning which are extant in their books'. Bacon left money to found a lectureship in history, but when he died in 1626 he had none.

It was early in the seventeenth century that 'The Backs' came under college ownership, and rough, swampy fields were gradually transformed into the beautiful lawns and tree-lined paths that we see today. St John's secured land beyond the river in 1610, laid out a bowling-green and a tree-lined 'long walk'. In 1612-13 Trinity secured from the town part of Garret Hostel Green and a field on the other side of the river, in exchange for £50, a farm, and other pieces of ground, the most important being Parker's Piece. The college had, in fact, begun to enclose and plant the common land across the river before this date.

The Perse School was founded when Stephen Perse, who died in 1615, left money to build a schoolhouse large enough for 100 boys, and a convenient house for a master and usher, together with an almshouse for six poor women who were to be single and upwards of 40 years of age.

In 1620, part of the gaol adjoining the Guildhall was used to confine witches, the remainder for other prisoners, with a debtors' hall on the north side. The prisoners must have endured appalling conditions, as the gaoler was not paid, but had to exist on fees and by selling ale. On market days, the town crier collected scraps of food for the prisoners, and a number of people bequeathed sums of money to be applied for their relief.

When James I visited Cambridge in 1615 he was entertained lavishly, and enjoyed the performance of a comedy so much that he returned a few months later to see it again. The Vice-Chancellor issued an order that no member of the university and no college servant should enter any smoking-house, inn, or tobacco shop during the king's stay. No one, under penalty of being sent down, was to take snuff in Great St Mary's Church or in the Hall of Trinity College. These orders were withdrawn as soon as the king had left the town.

To commemorate the king's visit, a statue of him, flanked by his queen Anne of Denmark and Prince Charles, was erected on the court side of Trinity Great Gate. They were carved in London from blocks of clunch from a local quarry, and have weathered badly. James I came again in 1624, and during this visit the marriage treaty between Charles and Henrietta Maria of France was ratified.

Many colleges had tennis courts, and Lady Paston, writing to her son William at Corpus in 1624, said 'Beware of violent tennising', and in 1626, 'Some do use to heat themselves very much with tennis and then drink burnt sack and such like.' Dr Walsall, the Master of Corpus, sought to allay her fears: 'I perceive your ladyship feared his excess at tennis though I am persuaded there is not any exercise more wholesome, and no many more gentleman like.' Duport, in some *Rules* for undergratuate written in about 1660 advised, 'Use Tennis sparingly, and never immediately after meals, it being too violent and too stirring.'

Students were still practising archery in 1629, as in that year an order made by the Corporation referred to 'Queens' College having often digged up sodds in the Green by Newnham for the repairing of their butts'.

King's built a two-arch bridge in 1627 at a point in the centre of the riverside path, the first college bridge to be built with stone. The Chapel of Peterhouse, the most striking building of the period, was begun in 1628 when Dr Matthew Wren was Master. He explained that it had been built because of the inconveniences arising from the use of a neighbouring church, the irksomeness of having to go outside the college walls in the winter time before sunrise, and after sunset in the evening, and the opportunity thereby afforded to the more disorderly members of extending their rambles through the town during the rest of the evening.

Milton was at Christ's 1625-32. Almost every guidebook to Cambridge mentions a mulberry tree planted by the poet in the college grounds. Actually this tree is no doubt the last one surviving of 300 planted by the college in 1608-9, when James I wished to promote the cultivation of mulberry-trees and had 12,000 distributed.

Plague raged in Cambridge from April to November in 1630. 'In the meane time our Universitie is in a manner wholly dissolved, all meetings and exercise ceasing; in many colleges almost none left.'

During the twelve years that Charles I ruled without a Parliament, his attitude towards the university was influenced by Laud. One of his first measures was to send a letter to the Chancellor, requiring him to ensure that the Vice-Chancellor and Heads of Colleges should restore the ancient discipline in the university. 'We, who are very desirous that at all times those nurseries of religion and learning should not in the least measure decline from their former integrities and reputations, may put our hand also thereunto, if there should be cause.'

There is a document annotated by Laud on 'certain disorders in Cambridge to be considered in my visitation'. It is dated 23 September 1636, and among other things it was alleged that 'M.A.s and Fellow Commoners do not attend public prayers, and dinner in hall, and frequent Taverns and Town Houses. Students do not wear clerical clothes, but new fashioned gowns of blue, green, red, or mixed colours; they have fair roses upon their shoes, wear long frizzled hair upon the head, broad spread bands upon the shoulders and long Merchants' Ruffs about the neck, with fair feminine cuffs at ye wrist. On Fridays and Fastdays Victualling Houses have good store of flesh. Tutors allow their pupils to draw double supper money to spend in the town, and the Proctors are bribed to allow this. Trinity College very negligent in their Chapell and prayers in it. Some Fellows never attend. . . . The choir is negligent and unskilful and negligent in their postures. Few bow at the name of Jesus and some turn to the West door at the creed. Services are scamped and mutilated. King's College quiremen cannot sing and are very negligent Choristers are half mute and come without surplices.'

Great St Mary's was used for two important annual ceremonies, the Comitia Priora, an examination for the Bachelor's Degree, beginning on Ash Wednesday, and the Comitia Maxima, for M.A. candidates, at the beginning of July. Tribunes were erected to accommodate the spectators and candidates had to state a proposition that they would be willing to defend. With a senior graduate called the Moderator presiding, an M.A. called the Prevaricator attacked the student's proposition. Some of these Disputations were profound and learned, an admirable test of a man's ability and knowledge, but in time they often tended to become irreverent and superficial.

A complaint made to Laud in 1636 alleged that the Prevaricators made profane and scurrilous jests to amuse the onlookers, and Dr Barlow, Master of Trinity 1672-77, protested that the church was 'deformed with scaffolds erected for the spectators and defiled with rude crowds and outcries'.

In 1639 the Bishop of Ely reported that the Chapels of Emmanuel, Sidney, and Corpus Christi had never been consecrated, and that most of the churchyards of Cambridge were annoyed and profaned with dwelling houses and shops, and part turned into gardens.

In 1637-8 a bitter quarrel, known as the Butt Close controversy, arose between King's and Clare. The latter's buildings were in such a poor state that they decided to rebuild, and wished to set back the new front range to give more light and air to both colleges, and provide a better view of King's College Chapel. In recompense, Clare wished to gain access to a field beyond the river which belonged to King's, and was used by their scholars for exercise and for the grazing of horses.

Opposite top: The Refectory of the Austin Friars, 1780, from a water-colour in Cambridge University Library. In the seventeenth century the building was used as a printing house, and since 1907 the site has been occupied by part of the Cavendish Laboratory.
Opposite bottom: The School of Pythagoras, 1783

The Refectory of St Augustins Monastery Cambridge
1780

King's would probably have agreed to this plan, but Clare petitioned the king, asking for a large piece of Butt Close. King's then said that they did not want to have the new buildings set back, as they would be more exposed to the winds. Some colleges kept many riding horses because they owned widely dispersed estates which had to be visited periodically, and King's said that they needed the field because they had to keep ten horses.

After a long and acrimonious dispute, Clare was allowed to rent a part of Butt Close, giving £100 as compensation, also £10 'to King's College Groomes or the children of such Groomes as suffered most losse by ye grasse of Butt Close being taken from them and parted wth to Clarehall'. In 1639-40, Clare built their beautiful stone bridge, the first in Cambridge in a classical style. The east and south range of the new court were completed, and the west range begun, until work was halted by the Civil War.

The Fellows' Building of Christ's, a large free-standing range of three storeys, with dormers above, and the first in Cambridge to have the upright type of window, was begun in 1640. Although it is the most important Cambridge building of the mid-seventeenth century, the designer is unknown.

A mid-seventeenth century tutor gave the following advice to undergraduates: 'Goe immediately from your Tutor's Chamber at night to your prayers, and retire to your devotions and reading the scriptures. Carry your self submissively and reverently towards your Superiours, by bareing the head, and bowing the body when you meet them. Let your garbe be grave and sober, and yet cheerful and pleasant. Sitt not up late at nights, noe not at your studies but goe to bed in time, and commonly at ten of the clock. Refraine foot-ball, it being as it is commonly used a rude, boistrous exercise, and fitter for Clownes then for Schollers. I am no great friend of going downe the water . . . some under colour of going a fishing, drop into a blind house and there drink like fishes.'

Opposite: John Nicholson, known as 'Maps', 1790. Gunning says that 'He was indefatigable in the pursuit of business, and was to be seen going from room to room in the different colleges, announcing himself by shouting MAPS as he proceeded'.

FIVE

From the Civil War
until 1750

Cambridge was of great military importance during the Civil War. It commanded the roads between East Anglia and the Midlands, and became the headquarters of the Eastern Counties Association formed to defend East Anglia. Oliver Cromwell had studied at Sidney, and in 1640 became one of the M.P.s for the town.

Two years later, Charles I visited Cambridge and asked the colleges to send him money and plate. Some was safely conveyed to York, but Cromwell intercepted another consignment. To improve the defences of the town he strengthened the fortifications at the castle, seizing materials intended for the new buildings at Clare. He destroyed all of the bridges except the Great Bridge, and built brick barracks for a garrison of about 300 men.

In February 1643, when there was a threat that the royal army might come, Cromwell raised a force of 30,000 men, and 1,000 remained when the threat had passed. Captured officers and ejected or suspect Fellows were kept under surveillance in the Old Court of St John's. King's Chapel served as a drill hall, colleges were obliged to give money to the Parliamentary cause, many Fellows were dismissed, and teaching was disrupted.

The university, in a petition to Parliament, said that 'Our Schools daily grow desolate, mourning the Absence of their Professors and their wonted Auditories ... frightened by the Neighbour Noise of War, our students either quit their Gowns, or abandon their Studies.'

Parliament ordered the removal of church furniture and decoration introduced under the influence of Laud and considered to offend against the principles of the Reformation. Altars, crucifixes, crosses, and images of the Trinity, the Virgin Mary, or saints had to be removed, and all organs demolished. Some colleges had anticipated these measures. The accounts of Trinity for 1642 record a payment 'To Chambers for not blowing ye organs for a whole Year' and 'To Mr. Jening for taking down ye Organ-pipes.' King's took down their organ, but retained the case.

In St John's, furniture was removed from the Chapel; the organ, pictures, and the cross on the tower taken down, and the walls whitened. The sepulchres of Fisher and Ashton became apartments, and the statue of St John on the gateway was removed. In Dr Wren's Peterhouse Chapel the Puritans were angered to find 'so much Popery in so small a chapel'.

The Earl of Manchester arrived in 1644 to purge the university of men with Royalist sympathies. Only those who suscribed to the Solemn League and Covenant which required zealous endeavour for the 'extirpation of Popery, Prelacy ... Archbishops, Bishops, Deans, Chapters, Archdeacons, and all that Hierarchy', were permitted to remain Masters or Fellows. Ten Masters were ejected and the Earl's agent, William Dowsing, destroyed altars, statues, etc. in the colleges, but glass was defaced only in Clare, Peterhouse, and Magdalene. After the Battle of Naseby in 1645, Royalist forces came within two miles of the town, but withdrew when Parliamentary troops marched out to oppose them.

The Small Bridges, which were among those destroyed, were rebuilt in 1648, but were only wide enough for one vehicle to pass at a time. The Civil War caused a complete disruption of the Anglican churches, and in 1649 only one parish had a minister, though there were preachers at Great and at Little St Mary's.

The Restoration caused further upheavals in the university, when men who had been imprisoned or dismissed regained their former positions. On 11 May, 1660, Charles II was proclaimed on the Market Hill by the Mayor and the Town Clerk, and on the following day by the university. 'The Vice-Chancellor and all the Doctors in Scarlet Gowns the Regents and the Non Regents and Bachelors in their hoods turned and all the Schollars in Capps went with lowd Musick before them to the Crosse on the Market Hill ... The Musicke brought them back to the Schooles again and there left them, and went up to the top of King's College Chapell, where they played a great while ... all ye soldiers were placed round on top of their Chapell, from whence they gave a volley of shott.'

The Act of Uniformity of 1662 compelled all dons to declare that they would adhere to the Anglican liturgy and that the Solemn League and Covenant was an illegal oath. The Quakers were persecuted, and in 1660, 67 members of the Society of Friends were in prison.

Among those who suffered during the Civil War was Dr Matthew Wren, Master of Peterhouse, and Bishop of Ely from 1638 to 1667. In 1642 he was imprisoned in the Tower of London because his high church practices had offended the Protestant laity, and he remained there for 18 years. While imprisoned he vowed that if he should regain his liberty and possessions he would build a church. On his release, he asked his nephew, Christopher Wren, to design a new chapel for Pembroke, and this was built in 1663-4. It was the architect's first completed work, and the first sacred building in England in the classical style. Five years later, Wren designed a new chapel with loggias for Emmanuel.

The third important building of Wren in Cambridge is Trinity College Library. Isaac Barrow, the Master, a brilliant mathematician, attempted to persuade the university to build a hall for important ceremonies. When they would not agree, as if to demonstrate what might be done, he built the Library, begun in 1676.

Wren originally suggested a domed circular building. The 150-foot long rectangular building, raised on columns with a cloister beneath, is one of Wren's masterpieces. For the interior he designed bookcases along the walls and at right angles to them, forming 30 study cubicles with a square table in each. The cases are adorned with exquisite carvings in limewood by Grinling Gibbons, and at the far end stands Thorwaldsen's statue of Byron. Intended for Westminster Abbey, but not accepted, the statue remained in the Custom House for about 12 years until it was given to Trinity.

The original buildings of St Catharine's were in a bad state, and it was decided to demolish all except a range to the north in Queens' Lane. The Hall and west and south ranges were completed by 1695, and the Chapel begun in 1703. Trinity and St John's remained the only large colleges for the 200 years from the Restoration until the middle of the nineteenth century.

*   *   *

The Fens north of Cambridge were a huge expanse of marshland intersected by wide but shallow rivers, and the Cam was tidal to within ten miles of the town. Between 1607 and 1653, both the university and the town opposed draining schemes because it was feared that the level of water in the river would fall, and the boats and barges which brought many commodities would no longer be able to reach the town.

The Earl of Bedford, who owned land in Thorney and Whittlesey, and 13 partners, formed a Company of Adventurers which commenced drainage operations in 1631 under the direction of the Dutch engineer Cornelius Vermuyden. The Old Bedford and New Bedford rivers, 12 miles long, were cut from the Ouse at Earith to Denver, where a large dam with gates was built in 1651 to keep out the tide. The town protested that 'Whereas of old ships from Newcastle were wont to make 18 voyages in the year to Cambridge with sea coal, now, since the blocking of the stream at Denver and the diversion of its waters to Earith, they can make but 10 or 12, whereby the price of fuel hath increased by half.'

Some of the larger coastal vessels were unable to pass through the gates at Denver, so the fenland lighter was evolved, 40 to 50 feet long and about 10 feet wide, with a flat bottom. With a load of 25 tons they drew only about $3\frac{1}{2}$ feet. Five or more coupled together were pulled by horses, assisted by a single square sail when the wind was favourable. Where boundary fences extended to the river, stiles were erected on the towpath, and the horses trained to jump them.

The grounds of the riverside colleges displaced wharves which moved to Quayside and the vicinity of the King's and Bishop's Mills. Horses towing the barges were banished from college grounds, so a gravel causeway on which they could walk was constructed in the middle of the river.

It was during the reign of Charles II that regular annual horse races, the first in England, were established at Newmarket, and the whole of the Court was frequently there for racing, hunting and hawking. On these occasions the leading men of the university waited upon the king with loyal addresses, and Cambridge sent its best theologians to preach.

Fabian Stedman, the inventor of change-ringing, was parish clerk of St Bene't's in about 1650, and in its ancient tower ringers were probably taught for the first time an organized system of changes. His

Tintinnalogia was published in 1667 and *Campanologia or Art of Ringing Improved* in 1677. In 1682 he became Master of the Society of College Youths, bellringers who were not for the most part collegians, although many students took part.

The first Cambridge to London coach began in 1653, the journey taking 15 hours. Turnpike trusts improved the roads after 1663, and from 1724 a number of Acts were passed to improve the roads to London and other places. Strype's *Letters* (1661) mention the lawlessness prevailing in the streets. 'Most intolerable robberies are hereabouts. In 2 or 3 days, 6 or 7 committed – 2 or 3 killed. Last sabbath within a mile a man knocked on the head. A scholar of Peterhouse both ears cut off because he told some thieves to whom he had given some money that if they found any more upon him they could inflict what punishment they liked upon him. So finding 20s. by searching they took him at his word and inflicted the cheater's punishment upon him.'

Punishments were severe. In 1664 a man tried for robbery refused to plead, and 'was sentenced to be and was pressed to death, one hour being taken for the process'. In 1663, when an Act for the better collection of excise duty was passed, it was stated that every college and hall in both universities 'did brew their own ale and beer within their own precincts and sizing it out to their own members within their own precincts were not liable to excise'.

The Settlement Law of 1662 governed the treatment of the poor for over 150 years. Parishes were responsible for the poor persons residing in them, and many paupers were hounded from place to place and sometimes given money to induce them to leave. In the seventeenth and eighteenth centuries, children of the poor were apprenticed at the age of 7 or 8.

From 1660 the representatives of the town in Parliament usually came from leading county families, and were chosen by the Mayor, Bailiffs and freemen, the electors numbering only about 100 in all. At every election there was fraud and bribery, and additional freemen were created to sway the voting. In 1737, 66 of the 248 voters were men who had become freemen only a month before the election.

There were two routes to London, one via Bishops Stortford, the other via Ware, but both roads were bad. Pepys often did the journey on horseback, usually taking two days. To do the journey in a single day he would start at 4 a.m. and arrive between 8 and 9 p.m.

In about 1675, the work of Isaac Barrow of Trinity was beginning to make mathematical studies so important that they later became the pre-eminent subject, and eventually the sole means of obtaining a high degree. Newton, who entered Trinity as a sub-sizar at the age of 19 in 1661, returned as a Fellow in 1667 and occupied the 'spiritual chamber' beside the Chapel, then from 1679-96 had rooms on the first floor north of the Great Gate. Here he wrote his *Principia Mathematica* (1687), made experiments with a prism bought at Sturbridge Fair, and worked out the principles of the theory of gravity.

Newton had a small garden between the college and the road. 'He was very curious in his garden, which was never out of order, in which he would seldome time take a short walk or two, not enduring to see a weed in it.' The Junior Bursar's accounts record a payment 'for mending the wall between Mr. Newton's garden and St. John's'. This wall was pulled down in 1856.

Newton was knighted in the Lodge in 1705 by Queen Anne. Pepys' *Diary* relates how Newton foretold a Dutch naval victory. 'Sir Isaac Newton came into the Hall of Trinity College and told the other Fellows that there had been an action just then between the Dutch and the English, and that the latter had the worst of it. Being asked how he came by this knowledge he said that, being in the observatory, he heard the report of a great firing of cannon, such as could only be between two great fleets, and that as the noise grew louder and louder, he concluded that they drew near to our coasts; and consequently that we had the worst of it, which the event verified.'

Oxford claims the first coffee house in England, opened in about 1650. Roger North, in his *Life* of his brother John, who entered Jesus in 1660, says that 'Whilst he was at Jesus College, coffee was not of such common use as afterwards, and coffee houses but young. At the time there was but one, kept by one Kirke . . . But now the case is much altered; for it is become the custom, after chapel, to repair to one or other of the coffee houses (for there are divers), where hours are spent in talking; and less profitable reading of newspapers . . . And the scholars are so greedy after news (which is none of their business), that they neglect all for it; and it is become very rare for any of them to go directly to his chamber, after prayers, without doing his suit at the coffee house; which is a vast loss of time grown out of pure novelty, for who can apply close to a subject with his head full of the din of a coffee house?'

In 1662, Henry Kirke of Little St Mary's parish was charged before the ecclesiastical court with selling coffee on a Sunday. The university authorities apparently agreed with North that students wasted too much time in coffee houses, and in 1664 it was decreed that men going to them without leave of their tutor should be punished.

Edmond Millar, in *An Account of the University of Cambridge and the Colleges There* (1675) wrote that 'The Coffee-houses are daily frequented, and in great Numbers of all sorts (the Heads of Houses and other Doctors excepted) at all Hours, especially Morning and Evening.' One of the early establishments was known as 'Greek's' because of the nationality of the owner. Dockerell's was famous for its milk punch. The Turk's Head was in Trinity Street, and John Delaporte's establishment next to Emmanuel was popular because it had a library of books, a pleasant garden, and musical performances. From 1700-25 the number increased greatly. They provided a wide range of beverages to a predominantly male clientele.

Early non-conformist meetings were held in a number of houses until, in 1687, the Presbyterians purchased ground on Hog Hill (Downing Place) and erected a meeting-house. The Rev. Jospeh Hussey persuaded a majority to adopt Congregationalism, but in 1696 a minority opposed to this joined the Congregational church in Green Street and eventually induced them to become Presbyterian. Another secession occurred in 1721 when about 100 left to found a Baptist community, fitting up a stable and granary beside the Spinning House.

In 1703 a subscription list was opened to establish schools for poor children, the boys to be taught reading, writing, and arithmetic, the girls to read, write, and sew. All were to be taught the catechism and had to go to church twice on Sundays. Sir Isaac Newton was an early contributor.

*   *   *

During the first third of the eighteenth century, Richard Bentley of Trinity was by far the most outstanding Master. He was the foremost critical scholar of classical learning of his time, and Macaulay said that he was 'the greatest man in his own department that has appeared in Europe since the revival of letters'. Appointed Master in 1700, he constructed an observatory on top of the Great Gate for Roger Cotes, the first Plumian Professor of Astronomy, and a laboratory for Vigani, Professor of Chemistry. It was largely due to Bentley that the university set up a printing press of its own in 1698. A printing-house was built in Queens' Lane and a Dutchman appointed 'Inspector of the Press'.

In spite of his great gifts as a scholar, Bentley had an exceedingly overbearing and truculent character, and he was in conflict with the Fellows for more than 40 years. He extended and embellished the Lodge, and spent a very large sum on the Chapel, erecting the screen, splendid panelling, and a noble Renaissance altarpiece with large Corinthian columns. To help to pay the cost, the Fellows were required to sacrifice a year's share of the college dividend.

In 1729 the Fellows brought 64 accusations against him. Legal arguments delayed the trial until 1732, when he was deprived of the mastership, but he continued to live in the Lodge for a further eight years until his death at the age of 80.

In 1715 there was a demonstration at Oxford in favour of the Stuarts, but Cambridge University sent an address to George I to assure him of their zeal and attachment to his person and government. The King, to show his appreciation, purchased the library of John Moore, Bishop of Ely, and presented it to the university. This collection of 30,000 volumes contained many rare books and manuscripts, and although the Library was enlarged, many books remained for some time in heaps on the floor. They were so inadequately guarded that several thousand were stolen.

The university decided to alter the Regent House to enlarge the Library, and to build a new Senate House. Sir James Burrough proposed a scheme for a three-sided court with the Senate House in its present position, an identical building opposite for the registry and printing-house, and a new library building linking the two wings.

The Senate House, designed by James Gibbs, was built between 1722-30, and during this time a number of people violently opposed the building planned for the south, on the grounds that it would mask the view of King's College Chapel. Dr Gooch, Master of Caius, led the protests, describing it as 'A scheme that will so effectually shut out all view of that noble fabrick King's Chappell, that I wonder how the University and that College can bear it; and a scheme so injurious to Caius College that I am fully resolved not to bear it.' The matter was taken to the courts, where proceedings lasted from 1727-30. The plans for a building to the south were eventually abandoned.

In 1723 Gibbs began the Fellows' Building at King's, and here again it was intended to complete the court by two other ranges, but these were not constructed.

Sir James Burrough was a distinguished amateur architect who designed the Fellows' Building at Peterhouse erected in 1738-42 and Clare College Chapel. Many of the college buildings in Cambridge, of clunch or rubble, were by now in a bad state of repair, and Burrough refaced some of them with stone Pembroke in 1712-17, Trinity Hall 1728-42, Gonville Court at Caius and Peterhouse just after the mid-century. Small Gothic windows (one of them can still be seen in a corner of the First Court of Trinity Hall) were replaced by larger sash windows.

The 'Backs' were transformed by Bentley in 1717-18, when 30 acres of marshy pasture were laid out with gravelled walks and avenues of limes and elms. Trinity paddocks were raised by depositing earth and rubbish on them; Bowtell says that surplus earth from eight churchyards was carted to the college grounds on the west of the river.

*   *   *

Defoe visited Sturbridge Fair in 1723 and described it as the greatest in the world. Goods from all parts of England and the Continent were displayed in booths arranged in rows like streets. The fair was first attended by hackney-coaches from London in 1605, and in Defoe's time 50 of these conveyed people to and from the town. From London, too, came wherries, transported on waggons, which were used to tow boats to the fairground. In 1744 it was stated that many hundreds of waggons passed through Godmanchester annually during the month of September on their way to the fair.

An account by Edward Ward describes the part of the fair occupied by booksellers, and show that shop-lifting was not unknown. 'Some that have no money come to buy books, whilst others, who want it, take 'em slily up, upon condition to pay if they're catch'd,' hiding the books in a gown sleeve. He describes the patter of a famous book auctioneer: 'Here's an old author for you, gentlemen, you may judge his antiquity by the fashion of his leather-jacket; herein is contained, for the benefit of you scholars, the knowledge of everything ... For your encouragement, gentlemen, I'll put him up at two shillings ... What? Nobody bid? ... Fye, for shame, why sure men of your parts and learning will never suffer the works of so famous an author to be thus undervalued ... What? nobody amongst you gentlemen of the black robe, that has so much respect for the wisdom of our ancestors, as to advance t'other threepence?'

There were colourful processions to proclaim the fair. Led by the Crier on horseback and dressed in scarlet, the Town Music of 12 players, supplemented for the occasion by three drums, two trumpets, and two French horns, was followed by numerous mounted officials, the Mayor in finery which had formerly belonged to the Lord Mayor of London, his horse richly caparisoned and led by two footmen called 'red-coats' who carried white wands. This procession was an annual event until 1758, and in a reduced form until 1790.

In 1701 the Mayor and Corporation gave a company permission to perform plays at the fair, but the university swore in 62 proctors who demolished the booth and imprisoned the celebrated actor Doggett, founder of the Thames Watermen's Badge.

The Vice-Chancellor issued an edict in 1730 stating that 'Whereas certain Players propose to Act Plays in an House erected near Paper Mills, and the Senate of the University have out of a just Resentment Discountenanced such Illegal Practices: I do hereby strictly charge and command all Scholars not to go There ... I do likewise forbid all under the Degree of Masters of Arts from going to Sturbridge Fair, without Consent of the Master or President of their particular College signified under his Hand Writing.' There followed particulars of the punishments to be given to offenders.

A playhouse established in 1737 was not allowed to open, but in spite of the enactment against theatrical entertainments, a London company performed a pantomime entitled *Harlequin's Frolics,* or *Jack Spaniard Caught in a Trap* in Hussey's Great Theatrical Booth in 1748.

The Disputations in Latin, which trained men to attack or defend an argument, were still important, but tended to decline after a Senate House Examination was instituted in about 1730. The papers consisted mainly of mathematical questions which could be answered in English, and after

1747 the results were printed. From 1752 the successful students were divided into wranglers, senior and junior optimes, and those who had merely qualified for a degree. The standard was low, because many of the undergraduates had not studied mathematics at school. There was so little demand for advanced teaching that many professors gave no lectures.

*   *   *

The usual route to London at this time was by the Old North Road via Ware. The Great North Road was not so important until the days of the stage coaches and the turnpike acts of the eighteenth century. Some of the very bad roads were improved by private benefactors. William Worts, dying in 1709, left money for 'the making of a Calcey or causeway from Emmanuel College to Hogmagog, alias Gogmagog Hills'. *Cantabrigia Depicta* (1763) says that 'William Worts, Esq., caused a causeway to be cast up to the Gogmagog Hills, 4 miles east of Cambridge, whither gentlemen ride out clean in the depth of winter.'

Cambridge can claim to have the first milestones to be erected in Great Britain since the Roman occupation. For about 150 years the income from the Mowse and Hare bequests was spent on filling up ruts in the road to Barkway. In 1725, Dr Warren, Vice-Master of Trinity Hall, decided to erect suitably inscribed milestones, measured from a disc cut in the southwest buttress of the tower of Great St Mary's, along this road. These milestones aroused great interest among travellers, and news about them spread afar. On 25 April 1728, when George II visited the university, the first stone was replaced by a Roman stone, 8 feet high. Dr Warren later decided to place milestones along other highways at his own expense.

The sluice gates at Denver, which had been destroyed in 1715 by a very high tide in a gale force wind, were rebuilt in 1749. From 1650 until the end of the eighteenth century, the Corporation and the university frequently complained to Parliament that the draining of the Fens had made navigation more difficult. They alleged that it had increased the price of coal, fish, and foreign goods coming from King's Lynn. In 1653 they said that prices had risen by one-third, and in 1777 it was alleged that the river trade with the counties of Bedford, Buckingham, and Huntingdon had been completely destroyed.

Nevertheless, lighters brought all manner of provisions from the Fenlands, including fish, wildfowl, butter and cheese. Owing to the lack of wood in the county, peat turves were cut and dried at Burwell and Reach and used as fuel. Sedge, a coarse growth of reeds, was also used extensively, and there was a Sedge Yard and Sedge Hall near Quayside. Every college had a sedge loft, and servants wore special gloves to protect their hands from the sharp edges of the sedge when they were lighting fires.

The growth of London in the eighteenth century provided a market for many products of the region, notably butter, which was sent from Cambridge by waggon. The town was an important distribution centre for many commodities, including corn, coal, malt, and fish.

Many of the more prosperous men in the town were innkeepers. According to Lyson's *Magna Britannia,* Cambridge had, in 1749, 156 inns and public-houses. Printers, booksellers, and stationers served the university, and a considerable number of craftsmen were employed in building for the colleges.

From early times, temporary galleries and platforms had been put up in Great St Mary's for university ceremonies, and permanent side-galleries were constructed in 1735. Masters of Arts sat below them on benches placed sidewise, and a huge octagonal pulpit, so high that the top was almost on the level of the galleries, was built in the centre of the nave. It had an interior staircase, and the preacher disappeared inside until the worshippers saw his head appear.

The Masters and Doctors were not satisfied with their seats in the chancel, and in 1754 a large gallery with seats in tiers was constructed across the whole width of the chancel and occupying half of its length. Cole called this 'Very absurd in design; both as the Doctors who sit there are generally old men, sometimes goutified, and not well able to get upstairs, and also are made to turn their backs on the Altar, which is not so decent, especially in an University.' Officially called the Throne, this structure was known to undergraduates as Golgotha, the Place of a Skull (Matthew XXVIII, 33), a punning allusion to it as the place of the Heads.

At St John's, in 1740, it was 'Ordered by the master and seniors, that if any scholar *in statu pupillari* shall, when the gates are shut by order of the master, break open any door, or by scaling of walls, leaping of ditches, or any other ways, get out of the limits of the college, he shall be *ipso facto* expelled . . That no scholars ever presume to loiter, or walk backwards and forwards in any of the courts or cloysters; and that when the names shall have been called over by order of the master, all depart quietly to their chambers, as they shall answer it at their peril.'

SIX

The Eighteenth Century, 1750-1800

A Shire-House had been built near the castle in the reign of Elizabeth, and in 1747 a new building was erected in front of the Guildhall on a site previously occupied by stalls. Two courts for the assizes and county sessions were constructed on pillars so that stalls could stand beneath.

James Essex, a local builder who worked for many of the colleges, rebuilt the Great Bridge in stone in 1754, and two years later began the riverside range in white brick for Queens'. The college intended to demolish the range of 1460 and extend Essex's work, and it is fortunate that the full scheme was abandoned, and that the picturesque early work remains. In 1770 Essex built the range of Emmanuel facing St Andrew's Street, and, in 1782, a new Guildhall with a large assembly hall, the cost being met by public subscription and the admission of a number of honorary freemen who each paid 30 guineas.

A project to enlarge the University Library was strongly supported by the Chancellor, the Duke of Newcastle, and the beautiful east front of the Old Schools was begun in 1755 according to plans by Burrough, although Stephen Wright made the elevations and supervised the construction. In 1760, the Rev. R. Walker bought the 'Mansion House' of 27 rooms and a great parlour 70 yards long which had been a part of the Austin Friary, and five acres bounded by Free School Lane, Corn Exchange Street, and Downing Street. He presented this property to the university, and the grounds became the Public Physic (Botanic) Garden.

In 1814 the Botanic Garden was described as 'conveniently disposed, and well-watered'. A handsome greenhouse was 'richly stored with curious exotics . . . some tea, coffee, and bread-fruit trees; a cotton tree;

and many others of equal curiosity and value'. A building for the lecturers in chemistry and botany was erected, and after the removal of the Botanic Garden in 1846-52, the site became of immense value to the university, as here the early scientific laboratories were erected.

Carter, describing Pembroke in 1753, said that 'The Master's Lodge, in a Ground Room he hath a Printing Press with the Apparatus belonging thereto, wherein he is printing his Astronomical Works. But the chief beauty of this Lodge is (in my opinion) the Gardens, and therein the Water-Works, contrived by the present Master (and here let me tell you he is a great Mechanic) which supplies a beautiful and large Basin in the middle of the Garden, and wherein he often diverts himself in a machine of his own contrivance, to go with the Foot as he rides therein.' He apparently anticipated the pedal-boats seen at the seaside and on pools today.

Carter was referring to Roger Long, Master 1733-70, an autocratic and quarrelsome man who was Professor of Astronomy. He built the first planetarium, a large tin sphere in which 30 person could sit, and by turning a handle, 'the relative situation and successive motions of the heavenly bodies' could be demonstrated. This sphere was destroyed by Waterhouse during the alterations made in the nineteenth century.

Carter tells us that at Trinity 'The Gardens and Bowling-Green are kept in excellent Order, especially the Vice-Master's Garden (who is a great Virtuoso in Flowers etc) where are abundance of Exotic Plants, Flowers, brought from both the Indies, and where is Annually raised a great Number of Anana's or Pine-Apples, in the greatest Perfection.'

Cantabrigia Depicta (1763) describing Queens', says 'The Gardens being very extensive, well planted with Fruit, and adorned with Rows of Elms, and fine Walks, make it a very agreeable Retirement for Students: And indeed this, and many of the Colleges of the University, are situate in the Country, in a Manner, far removed from the Noise and Hurry of the Town.' The author lamented the poor town buildings: 'But the Misfortune of it here, as well as at Oxford, is, that none care to lay out much Money on College-leases; which is the true Reason the private Buildings are not equal to those in some other Towns.'

Carter gives details of a number of almshouses, some supported by colleges, then in existence, such as St Botolph's: 'In this parish I find 8 almshouses (belonging to Queens' College) for as many poor widows,

Opposite top: *Nevile's Court Trinity College, by R. B. Harraden, Junr, 1809*
Opposite bottom: *Cambridge from the first milestone, Trumpington Road, 1809*

where each have their dwelling, two shillings a week, 20s. at Sturbridge Fair, 30 bushels of coal every winter, and two of them have sevenpence halfpenny a-piece in lieu of a Sunday dinner they used to have from the said college.' Life in the small parish workhouses was squalid and promiscuous. In the 1760s, many poor people were boarded out; in 1761 Great St Mary's boarded out some of the workhouse poor for 1s. 8d. a week.

Thomas Gray, the poet, went first to Peterhouse, but migrated to Pembroke after fellow-students had made him the victim of a practical joke. He feared that drunken students might cause a fire, and wrote to his friend Wharton on 9 January 1756 to ask him to buy for him 'a rope ladder, for my Neighbours every day make a greater progress in drunkenness which gives me reason to look about me ... I suppose it must have strong hooks or something equivalent a-top to throw over an Iron bar to be fixed within the side of my window'.

Some of his neighbours, knowing about his fears, shouted 'Fire' in the night, and Gray descended the rope ladder in his nightshirt into a bath of water which they had placed below his window. He spent most of the remainder of his life in Cambridge. Shy and retiring, he was horrified at the behaviour of some of the students who 'placed women upon their heads at noonday', rioted in the town, and ran up heavy bills at inns and coffee houses which they had no intention of paying. Professors and Fellows held nightly orgies at the Three Tuns Tavern, and Gray often found life in Cambridge almost intolerable.

Alexander Cruden, the compiler of the Concordance to the Bible, was another critic of Cambridge behaviour. He was a stern and somewhat eccentric moralist who styled himself 'The Corrector'. In 1755 he circulated an Address to the university and town beginning 'It is the opinion of the Corrector that the Sabbath is not observed by many people in Cambridge according to the Fourth Commandment. Many do not attend public worship, and many stand in an idle manner at their doors. Many ladies and gentlemen, after public worship is over, pass their time in Clare Hall Walks.'

A don of Emmanuel, Mr Neville, relates that Cruden was taken 'to some of ye Bawdy Houses at Barnwell, where by ye bye he did more service in a quarter of an hour than most of us preachers would do in a twelve month, for he talked to one of ye naughty ones in so solemn a

Opposite top: The original Botanic Garden, by W. Westall, from R. Ackermann's **History of the University of Cambridge,** 1815
Opposite bottom: The Prison and the Castle from the Huntingdon Road, by W. Westall from R. Ackermann's **History of the University of Cambridge,** *1815*

manner with such an Air of Gravity that he brought her at last to her Tears'.

Until 1769, students wore round caps of black cloth lined with silk or canvas, with a brim of black velvet for pensioners and silk for sizars. In June 1769 they petitioned the Chancellor, the Duke of Grafton, asking to be allowed to wear square caps, stating that they wished to attend the approaching installation of his Grace in a dress more decent and becoming. The Duke informed the university that the square cap might be adopted.

Robert Robinson, an eloquent preacher, became the minister of the Baptists in 1761. The congregation of about 20 met in barns and old buildings, but his preaching soon attracted larger numbers, and a new church was erected in 1764. His evening services were attended by about 200 undergraduates. His successor, from 1790-1806, Robert Hall, was even more gifted and influential. The Quakers, who had been holding services in a house in Jesus Lane, built a meeting-house in 1777.

Gunning writes that in 1788 'Almost every evening during the latter part of this winter there were riotous assemblages, and the windows of the dissenters were broken. A very large mob collected one evening who after breaking several windows, did great injury to the Meeting-house. They were headed by two chimney-sweepers, under whose direction they proceeded to the market-place and attacked several houses, trying to burst open doors: this was prevented by some M.A.s who assisted the town magistrates. By their united efforts the rioters were dispersed, but not before the Riot Act had been read. Several dissenters, fearing for their safety, went to America.'

The road to Ely was a roundabout route of over 20 miles via the causeway at Aldreth. By river it was much less, and in the eighteenth century regular boats pulled by horses ran daily. The *Cambridge Chronicle* of 27 November 1762, gave details of 'The new projected road between Cambridge and Ely to begin at the southwest corner of St. Giles churchyard, through Milton . . . to Lamb corner, Ely.'

The first modest building of Addenbrooke's Hospital was opened in 1766. John Addenbrooke, a Fellow of St Catharine's, dying in 1719 had left money to provide a hospital for the poor, but financial and legal difficulties had delayed the project. Additional funds were subscribed by the university and gentlemen of the borough and the county.

On the underside of the lintel of staircase G in the First Court of St John's are painted the words 'STAG, NOV. 15, 1777'. On that day, members of the college who were leaving the Hall after dinner were alarmed to see a number of sportsmen riding into the college in pursuit of a stag. First sighted at Chesterford, it had been chased for several hours, and eventually came to the backs of the colleges, crossed the river, and ran through the streets until it entered the college and took refuge in the staircase.

Gunning describes Commencement Sunday in 1785: 'The college walks were crowded. Every Doctor in the University wore his scarlet robes during the whole day. All the noblemen appeared in their splendid robes, not only at St. Mary's and in the college halls, but also in the public walks. Their robes (which are now uniformly purple) at that time were of various colours, according to the tastes of the wearers, – purple, white, green, and rose-colour, were to be seen at the same time. The people from the neighbouring villages then never ventured to pass the rails which separate the walks from the high road.'

A Plain and Friendly Address to the Undergraduates of the University of Cambridge (1786) complained of the waste of money on fashionable buckles, coats, or waistcoats, through the 'artful' civility of the accommodating shopkeeper'. In *Remarks on the Enormous Expense in the Education of many young men in the University of Cambridge* (1788) it was said 'that the Dress of the Undergraduates be taken into most serious consideration: being in its present State, Indecent, Expensive, and Effeminate'. Refrence was made to the high cost of riding: 'A Horsekeeper, one James Barrow, who in 1773 was not worth £10, died in 1786 worth £3,000 which he had acquired by letting and selling horses to the young men of the University.'

A bookseller, John Nicholson, universally known as 'Maps,' was one of the best-known characters of the town, and his portrait hangs in the University Library. Born in 1730, he began business by selling maps and prints from a small movable stall, and loaded with books he went from college to college crying out 'Maps, sir', whence the nickname. He later lived in a large old house adjoining the Provost's Lodge in King's Parade, where he had an extensive stock of books required for the college lectures, and established a circulating library. It was said that almost every student became a subscriber, and he also provided manuscript sermons and

various literary compositions. His son and grandson continued th
business, and when the buildings on the west side of King's Parade wer
pulled down, the former rebuilt and moved to the premises at the corne
of Trinity Street now occupied by Bowes & Bowes.

Until the end of the eighteenth century, Market Street was so narrov
that no vehicles could pass through. The fronts of the houses were then se
back three to four feet to allow single carts to pass.

R. Master, in his *History of Corpus Christi* (1753) said that the practic
of digging up human bodies in the churchyards of Cambridge and
neighbouring villages and carrying them into colleges to be dissected
became more common. A body brought by the 'resurrectionists' in 1768
was recognised to be that of Laurence Sterne, who had studied at Jesus. I
had been buried in St George's, in the Bayswater Road, London, but had
been removed two days later.

*　　*　　*

Every undergraduate was placed under the care of a tutor who was in
charge of his education and behaviour and his financial affairs. In early
days, most tutors supervised only two or three men, but more as the
number of freshmen increased. The number of new entrants varied widely
from year to year; at Trinity in 1655, 53 men were admitted by twelve
tutors, and in 1715 fourteen men by six tutors. For about a hundred years
from 1755 there were only two tutors. They lectured to their pupils,
collected their fees and ensured that they paid their bills.

During the eighteenth century, discipline in the university was slack,
and the general level of scholarship low. Political loyalty or family
connections gave dons a better chance of promotion than sound
scholarship or duties conscientiously performed, and the financial
rewards were so meagre that clever men left to enter the church or the
professions. Major attention was given to mathematical studies, and other
subjects neglected. Many of the Fellows were men of low birth who had
entered college as sizars; they were often coarse in their habits, and a
narrow monastic life led to drunkenness. Although most were in holy
orders, few appeared to have any deep religious convictions.

Some Fellows held several church livings and spent little time in
college. One or two tutors in each college did most of the teaching, and

many professors gave no lectures. Richard Watson became professor of Chemistry in 1764 and Professor of Divinity in 1771, but knew nothing of these subjects when he was appointed, though he studied to master them. He had entered Trinity as a sizar in 1754, and in his autobiography said that 'I had at the time of being elected a scholar been resident in college for two years and seven months, without having gone out of it for a single day.'

Although there were many rich men's sons at the university, noble families did not usually send their sons to Oxford or Cambridge, but engaged private tutors and sent them on the Grand Tour. The titled pensioners were called Fellow-Commoners and they dined at the high table with the Fellows, wearing coloured gowns richly trimmed with gold or silver lace, their caps cornered with velvet, and with tassels. They did not come to study and it was said that they 'be of no use to anyone but the Bedmaker, Tutor, and Shoe-Black'.

In 1786, disputes having arisen concerning the conferring of degrees in right of nobility and without an examination, it was decided that the following categories of persons qualified: Privy Councillors, Bishops, Dukes, Marquises, Earls, Viscounts, Barons, and the sons of noblemen; persons related to the king and the eldest son of such persons. Baronets and Knights might receive an M.A. Degree.

Religious questions were a chief topic of conversation between the more serious students. Among the leading 'Saints', as the Evangelicals were called, were two remarkable men, Isaac Milner and Charles Simeon. Milner was a poor boy who entered Queens' as a sizar in 1770. He graduated as Senior Wrangler with the distinction 'incomparabiles' because he was so superior to all others. He became a Fellow, Tutor, took priest's orders and was rector of St Botolph's. He studied chemistry, was elected a Fellow of the Royal Society when only 30, and in 1783 became the first Jacksonian Professor of Natural Experimental Philosophy. In 1791 he was appointed Dean of Carlisle and spent about a third of his time there; in 1792 he became Vice-Chancellor.

Charles Simeon entered King's in 1779, became a Fellow and vicar of Holy Trinity Church. At first he was unpopular because he was accused of preaching Methodism, and many gownsmen went to the church to cause disturbances. He continued his ministrations courageously, and after some years he had large congregations, half of them students. 2,536 of his sermons, in full or in outline, were eventually published in 21 volumes.

At King's he exerted a great influence. Although Cambridge educated half of the future Church of England clergy, there were no theological colleges and the university provided no official instruction in theology. In his rooms over the archway in the Fellows' Building, he held tea parties at 6 p.m. on Fridays to give instructions to men who wished to be ordained.

A group of the more thoughtful and earnest undergraduates known as 'The Apostles' began to meet in about 1820 to discuss literary and philosophical questions. Tennyson and F. D. Maurice were members. A Friendly Society for Promoting Useful Knowledge was established in 1784. The members, limited to 50 and mainly leading business men of the town, met weekly at the Black Bull Hotel. The Society was commonly known as The Bull Book Club and eventually had a library of 2,000 volumes. It was dissolved in 1841.

Theatres were banned, so Cambridge people had to be content with other amusements. Thus, in 1784, 'By permission of the Reverend the Vice-Chancellor: At the Concert Room at the Black Bear this present Friday evening, Mr. Cresswick will repeat a serious and comic lecture. The first part contains a few observations introductory to the recital of Collin's classical and beautiful 'Ode on the Passions', the very interesting and pathetic narrative of Damon and Pythias, and several striking passages from Shakespeare and other dramatic writers, after which, as a lighter amusement, he will deliver a lecture upon Hearts, the whole to conclude with a dramatic jeu d'esprit in imitation of Shakespeare's Seven Ages.'

Gunning tells us that the two hundredth anniversary of the foundation of Emmanuel was celebrated on 29 September 1784 by a magnificent entertainment. For several days previous, people were allowed to see turtles intended for the feast in tubs of water at the Master's Lodge.

In 1785 there was a proposal to make a canal from the upper river to join the Stort at Bishop's Stortford, from whence it would be possible to reach London, but the scheme was abandoned. Wordsworth entered St John's in 1787, and found that as he had studied mathematics at school, he was a year ahead of other Freshmen. From 1640 until about 1785, St John's had been the largest college, but henceforth Trinity took first place. Gunning, writing about Trinity Fellows in 1787, said that 'The Rev. James Backhouse B.D., like most of the Seniority, was considered a man of gallantry; but Cambridge not being the scene of his amours, he was not thought so immoral as the rest.'

For most of the eighteenth century there was little improvement in lighting the streets, and in 1751 it was stated that torches carried by students and linksmen terrified people lest houses be set alight. Some people maintained that better lighting would lead to more fights between persons who now passed without recognising one another in the darkness. It was also said that it was futile to put up more lamps because the students so often smashed those already installed.

Gunning says: 'To me (who have a perfect remembrance of all its horrible discomforts) it seems surprising that any family should have resided at Cambridge who could live anywhere else. The undergraduates when encountered in our dark streets were scarcely less ferocious than the members of the "Mohock and Sweating Clubs". Persons carrying dark lanterns, which were at that time called "bulls' eyes" were always insulted and their lanterns generally taken from them.'

'The wretched state of the streets had long been a disgrace to the University and Town of Cambridge. The gutters were in the middle of the streets, in several of which it was impossible for two carriages to pass each other, on account of the encroachments that had been made. Along the whole front of Pembroke College was a water-course, which divided the street into two very unequal parts: the west side was, by necessity, the carriage-road, but was only one-third the width of the road which adjoined the college, and was appropriated to foot-passengers.' Strangers sometimes mistook the wider road for the carriage-road, and accidents occurred, so soon after 1794 the channel was filled in, and the water diverted to the two runnels now on both sides of the road, and which never fail to intrigue visitors.

In 1788 the royal assent was given to 'An Act for better paving, cleansing, and lighting the Town of Cambridge, for removing and preventing obstructions and annoyances, and for the widening the streets, lanes and other passages within the said town.' One section of the Act anticipated the waiting restrictions of the present day: 'That after the said Twentieth Day of May, any Cart, Waggon, Dray, Hand Cart, or other Carriage shall be left to stand or continue in any Street, Lane, or publick Way in the said Town, or, in any Part or Parts thereof, with or without Horses or other Carriage let to hire, shall be left to stand or remain in any of the Streets, Markets, Lanes, Passages, or Places aforesaid, without horses, for any longer time than shall be necessary for setting down Passengers and for the loading or unloading of their Baggage, the same not to exceed one hour at any one time. Also all tradesmen's wares.' No cart must be driven faster than a footpace or without someone leading the horse.

A body of Paving (later Improvement) Commissioners was set up and empowered to cleanse, pave, and light the town and to levy rates, and it functioned for 100 years. Oil-lamps affixed to the walls of colleges and houses were first lighted on 18 September 1788, and Petty Cury was the first street to be paved with rounded cobbles. It was opened on the evening of 25 October 1788 by the surveyor and workmen, who with lighted torches and a band of music paraded the streets, after which the workmen supped together at the Wrestlers' Inn. By 1793 the paving of the town was completed, the Commissioners having expended £23,814 9s. $2\frac{1}{4}$d.

Buildings in front of the University Library were demolished, Trumpington Street was widened near Great St Mary's, and Senate House Passage constructed. A design by Sir John Soane for a building opposite the Senate House was rejected in 1791, as many people still considered that it would obscure the view of King's College Chapel.

Two notable undergraduate dining clubs were founded in the middle of the eighteenth century: The Beefsteak Club, its members limited to 11, who wore a uniform of a blue coat, buff waistcoat with 'B.S.' buttons, black trousers and white scarf, with a bull's head pin, and the The True Blue Club of 9 members, who wore a blue double-faced uniform, yellow buttons engrossed 'T.B.', and a buff waistcoat with a blue binding. The rules stated that 'No member to be considered in his uniform without black silk breeches and silk stockings. Dress wigs be worn by the members at the meetings of the club.' One one occasion the 7 members and 17 guests drank 67 bottles of wine.

The famous quarter-hour chimes of Great St Mary's were composed and installed by the Rev. J. Jowett, Fellow and Tutor of Trinity Hall, probably assisted by W. Crotch, a noted musician, in 1793. They were copied incorrectly at the Royal Exchange in 1845, and correctly in 1859 for Big Ben at Westminster, also for the cathedrals of Durham, Lincoln, and Wakefield, the Town Halls of Bradford and Manchester, and many other clocks throughout the English-speaking world. Unfairly to Cambridge, where they had originated, they are often called the Westminster Quarters.

Stage coaches had linked Cambridge with London since 1653, and by 1796 six coaches went there. The Royal Mail Coach for four passengers set out from the Sun Inn opposite Trinity every night at 11, arriving at the Bull and Mouth Inn near St Paul's at 6.30 a.m. The Cambridge Diligence for three passengers plied between the Hoop Inn and the White Horse Inn, Fetter Lane, and The Fly, with four passengers, between the Rose Inn and the George and Blue Boar, Holborn.

Prior's Stage Coach for six passengers plied between the Red Lion and the Bull in Bishopsgate Street, Hobson's Stage Coach, also for six, between the Blue Boar and the Green Dragon in Bishopsgate Street, and a Night Post Coach, which was guarded, took four passengers between the Eagle and Child and the Golden Cross, Charing Cross.

Five coaches went to places other than London. The waggons of James Burleigh, successor to Hobson, went to London on five days a week, also to other towns, and in 1798, during the war with France, he offered to loan to the Government 60 horses and eight waggons. In 1803, when it was feared that Napoleon might invade East Anglia, Robert Marsh & Sons offered to lend at an hour's notice 100 horses, 12 broad-wheel waggons, 24 flat-bottomed boats with the men and horses employed with them, four blacksmiths with a portable forge, two wheelwrights and two collar-makers. This offer was accepted.

Carts went to nearby towns, and waggons to places as far away as Lynn, Doncaster, and Sheffield. One carrier advertised that he could forward goods to Kendal, Newcastle, and any part of Scotland with the greatest care and safety.

*   *   *

From about 1784 until his death in 1816, John Mortlock III was the dictator of the town, and although it was a benevolent dictatorship there was much corruption and inefficiency. His grandfather came from a Pampisford family, and by 1725 he had a house in Cambridge. Three of his daughters married dons, and his son, John Mortlock II, amassed a large fortune from a drapery business near the Rose Inn. John Mortlock III married the heiress of a wealthy grocer, and in 1778, when he was only 23, took the first step towards becoming the powerful man in the town when he purchased the freedom of the borough. He became a councillor in 1780, and an alderman in 1782. In 1780 he founded, in the draper's shop, the first Cambridge bank, and removed it in 1783 to the 'Mansion House', formerly part of the Austin Friary and then in a ruinous condition, which he bought from the university. The bank was a boon to gentlemen and shopkeepers who need no longer send money to London and risk thefts by highwaymen.

Between 1787 and 1809 he was Mayor every other year, and in the other years served as deputy Mayor to one of his sons, a business partner, or a dependant. He was Mayor 13 times, and during his reign many charitable funds disappeared and much property belonging to the town of immense potential value was sold or let at low rents to members of the Corporation and their friends.

He formed a close association with the Duke of Rutland, Charles Manners, son of the Marquis of Granby whose popularity as a successful general caused numerous inns to be named after him. The Rutland family acquired a large estate at Cheveley and entertained lavishly, and when Pitt became Prime Minister, the Duke of Rutland was appointed Lord Lieutenant of Ireland.

Mortlock, then aged 29, was returned unopposed to Parliament, and for a short time before he resigned his seat in 1788 he was at the same time Mayor, Recorder, and M.P. for Cambridge. Rutland nominees were always returned unopposed. Mortlock founded the Rutland Club which met at the Eagle in Bene't Street, and here he and his friends planned their national and local political campaigns. Magistrates, councillors, and freemen who supported the Rutland interest were entertained to suppers and dinners.

In 1784, 24 new pro-Mortlock freemen were created on the pretext of raising money for a new town hall, and in 1789, 89 additional freemen, most of them Rutland dependants who did not live in Cambridge, but who could be brought in to vote if his rule were threatened. As a business man he was honest, and was banker to the university, but he boasted that he played with men as others moved chessmen on a board. To a friend who criticised him he said that 'Without influence, which you call corruption, men will not be induced to support government, though they generally approve of its measures.'

Mortlock had seven sons. The eldest was nine times Mayor, and the fth son five times. For 16 years after his death, corruption and the quandering of Corporation property continued unchecked.

During the summer of 1795 mobs frequently assembled to protest bout the high price of provisions. One seized a lighter laden with flour nd was about to divide the cargo among them when the Earl of Hardwick and some magistrates arrived and persuaded them to disperse, ut on the following morning they gathered in the market and insisted pon meat being sold for 4d a lb.

On 20 July 1795, the Vice-Chancellor and the Deputy Mayor ublished a notice: 'Information has been given us that butcher's meat, oultry, eggs, vegetables and other articles as are purchased in the public Market are there immediately sold again at an advanced price, to the reatest injury of the poor, and others resorting thereto. Therefore it is orbidden to sell anything in the Market until a bell rings.'

In 1790 the town gaol was removed to a building behind the Spinning House, and in 1802 the *Gentleman's Magazine* reported that 'Cambridge Town Bridewell is surrounded by a wall 15 feet high. The Keeper's alary was £30 from Hobson's Charity and £5 from the University. There were three cells for men, 9 feet x $7\frac{1}{2}$ feet, ventilated by an iron rating, with straw on the floor and a tub "served all necessaries". Each ell had a mattress, two blankets and a rug. There were ten cells for women and four courtyards with a privy in each. Many of the cells were n bad repair and dirty, and there was only one pump.'

Byron was at Trinity from 1805-8, a rebel who vented his dislike of lons and students in some of his verses, and referred to Cambridge as 'the lark asylum of a vandal race'. George Pryme wrote: 'It was during this visit that I saw a little of Lord Byron, who was then a nobleman at Trinity College, I used to sit opposite him at the Fellows' table ... He was unaffected and agreeable, but we Fellows did not think him possessed of any great talent, insomuch that when the *English Bards and Scotch Reviewers* appeared without his name, Monk and Rose and I would not believe that *he* was the author.'

Coleridge, at Jesus 1790-92, looked back on his college days with deep affection, though he must have sometimes been a trial to the authorities, as when he burnt the words 'Liberty and Equality' on the lawn with gunpowder. In 1803, when a French invasion was feared, the university formed a corps of volunteers 180 strong, and the future Lord Palmerston was one of the officers.

Colleges had their own barber, who in the early morning awakened students and shaved them. One of the most celebrated was Robert Foster known as the Cambridge Flying Barber, who died in 1799. For many years he was hairdresser to Clare, and was so esteemed that gentlemen of the university subscribed to buy him a silver basin. It was considered an honour to have been shaved in Foster's basin.

John Jacklin, who died in 1825, presided for many years over a society called 'The Sixteen' by whom he was called 'The Major'. After his death, the following note was found in his comb drawer: 'To Him whom these presents shall come Greetings. KNOW YE that JOHN JACKLIN alias THE MAJOR, though no pugilist, has every day a *brush* and *set-to*, and was frequently in the *suds;* for he entered great men's houses, and *sans cérémonie* took them by the nose, and *cut-off* more of their hairs than any disease or entail. Bees never harmed him, though he handled the *comb*. He was a staunch Tory, and brought many a *Wig* to the block: though a Sexagenarian, he was always daily at sweet "Sixteen", and although he sometimes met with *great* men, he was always acknowledged as "the Major".'

In about 1800 drunkenness was rife, and it was said that only three of the eight seniors in Trinity had a good character. The galleries of the Senate House frequently had to be cleared because students hissed and hooted derisively.

Benjamin Flower, printer of the *Cambridge Intelligencer,* was the first man to introduce leading articles in a provincial newspaper. In 1799 he was summoned to appear before the House of Lords for breach of privilege in commenting upon the action of a bishop; he was fined £100 and sentenced to six months' imprisonment in Newgate.

SEVEN

The Early
Nineteenth Century

Grantchester Meadows were acquired by King's in 1798 when they offered easy terms to their tenants at Grantchester and Coton if they would bear the cost of obtaining an Act of Parliament for dividing and allotting the open and commonable fields, commonable land and waste grounds within those parishes. George Pryme says that when he arrived in Cambridge in 1799, the villages all around were unenclosed. 'From the Backs of the Colleges in the direction of Coton was one vast plain. Towards Ely it was quite open, and when halfway to it, I roused wild duck as I rode along ... Between How House and Fenstanton, 9 or 10 miles from Cambridge, the fields were quite open, and rye, which the soil suited, was the corn mainly grown on them.'

In 1801 the built-up area of the town was only about one mile long and half a mile wide, and the population 9,276. Christopher Wordsworth says that in 1802 there were 632 undergraduates, of whom 117 were at St John's. In 1815 there were only about 2,000 university students in the whole of England.

Britton and Brayley wrote that 'The streets are, in general, narrow and winding, and the houses ill-built and crowded closely together ... The population compared with the limited extent of the town is very great ... Very little trade of any kind is carried on at Cambridge but that connected with the University.' The town had not been able to expand because it was hemmed in by the Barnwell Field, extending from the river beyond Jesus and round the eastern part of the town to Coe Fen, and by the Western Field between Huntingdon Road and Barton Road.

The Enclosure Acts for the Western Field in 1802 and for the Eastern

in 1807 caused the most significant topographical changes since th
fifteenth century. The Acts extinguished commoners' rights in respect o
much arable and pasture land encircling the town.

Sturbridge Fair was still important, the principal commodities sol
being wool, hops, leather, iron, and cheese, although it had decline
because the introduction of turnpike roads and canals had facilitate
commercial transactions in other parts of the country. In 1802 a false fir
alarm in the wooden Sturbridge Theatre caused a panic; five persons wer
trodden to death and many others injured. It was demolished in 180(
because it was thought to be unsafe. Charles Humfrey put up an inferio
building adjoining the Sun Inn in 1808, and in 1815 Wilkins erected th
existing buulding which became the Festival Theatre. Named the Theatr
Royal, it opened only during the vacations. Famous actors like Macready
Kemble, and Sheridan Knowles appeared there.

A guide book of 1814 says that the markets of Cambridge wer
'supplied in the most abundant manner with every article of provision: th
quantities that are exposed for sale are sometimes astonishing, and it
quality is in general excellent . . . Great quantities of fruit are brought, i
their season, from Ely and the villages . . . insomuch that, though ver
little fruit is grown in the town, no place in the world can be mor
plentifully supplied with it'.

The Shire Hall facing the market place was 'a modern handsom
structure' . . . but the Town Hall behind it 'from its obscure and confine
situation, scarcely ever seen, except by those who have business to transac
with it'.

'Owing to its advantageous situation, at the head of inland navigatio
from Lynn, it unavoidably secures an extensive trade in coals and corn
particularly oats and barley. Great quantities of oil, pressed by th
numerous mills in the isle of Ely, from flax, hemp, and cole-seed, ar
brought up the Cam. . . . A great quantity of butter is likewise conveye
every week from Norfolk and the Isle of Ely, and sent by the Cambridg
waggons to London, where it obtains the name of Cambridge butter.
The bargees were stalwart men who loved a fight, and there wer
undergraduates who equally welcomed occasions for displaying wit
them their pugilistic skills.

In 1808, Joseph Lancaster, a member of the Society of Friends
lectured in the Town Hall on public elementary education and explaine

the system used at his school in London. The disused meeting-house of the Friends in Jesus Lane became a school until larger premises were built at Castle End ten years later. Known as The New Free School, it had a spacious room for 300 boys between the ages of 6 and 11, and the annual expense for each pupil was said to be not quite 8s., including books, slates, etc. In 1815 the population of the town was about 10,000, but there were only 450 children in the charity schools.

Another early attempt to educate poor children was the establishment of the Jesus Lane Sunday School. On a Sunday morning in 1827, five undergraduates were sitting in a summer-house in Tennis Court Road when one of them remarked that 'It seems a pity that we do not spend part of our time in Sunday teaching.' They decided to start a Sunday School for Barnwell children in the Friends' Meeting House, and the success of this school led to the founding of others.

A teacher at the King Street School wrote in 1845: 'I have taught in Irish cabins, military tents in Egypt, in Syria, in English log-houses in America, the garrets of London, booths at races in Scotland – both black and white, slaves and freemen, and do not recollect any set of boys more difficult to teach than those of Cambridge.'

The establishment of charity schools caused the Perse School to lose many of its potential scholars, and Britton and Brayley, writing in 1831, said that 'The administration of this charity appears to be attended with some degree of mismanagement: the salaries are paid without being earned; and the School-house exists without scholars; for the few boys that sometimes receive their lessons at the master's lodge cannot be deserving of that title.'

In 1816 the building was let to the university for storing the Fitzwilliam collection, which remained there until 1842. In 1841 a new scheme of management was drawn up, the buildings were altered, and the number of pupils rapidly increased. In 1890 the premises in Free School Lane were sold to the university, and new school buildings erected in Hills Road.

In 1808 Lawrence Dundas, an undergraduate, after a drunken orgy in Bridge Street, was making his way to Barnwell when he fell into a ditch on Parker's Piece and, being too drunk to extricate himself, was found dead from exposure the next morning. The Rev. F. H. Maberley, in a pamphlet on *The Melancholy and Awful Death of Lawrence Dundas, undergraduate of Trinity College, Cambridge* said that 'Drunkenness is making gigantic strides in the University; the state of it, in this respect, is quite appalling. Again, with regard to women of the town . . . I have seen them parading the streets in the most impudent manner, accosting many that they meet and in some cases walking and talking with Universitymen in a drunken state, the latter of whom I have with difficulty sent to their college, and the women to their abode. One evening after 8 – in less than five minutes, two prostitutes met me, ran against me, and separated; two more came behind me and pushed against me, and two more ran hallooing by me.'

The Proctors could arrest any woman suspected of being a prostitute if found with an undergraduate in the streets. She was taken to the Spinning House, tried in private by the Vice-Chancellor, and imprisoned there. Carter says that 'The Bridewell (called by the inhabitants the Spinning House) is pleasantly situated near the fields at the south end of the parish of Great St. Andrew's, and is chiefly used for the confinement of such lewd women as the Proctors apprehend in houses of ill fame: though sometimes the Corporation send small offenders thither, and the crier of the town is often there to discipline the ladies of pleasure with his whip.'

Undergraduates were still obliged to submit to a narrow discipline. Few of the Masters were outstanding, yet they wielded immense power and opposed reforms. When, in 1811, some undergraduates wished to establish a branch of the British and Foreign Bible Society, the authorities opposed the proposal because it was thought that the young men should not concern themselves with such matters. In 1817 the Vice-Chancellor suppressed the Union (Debating) Society because political subjects were being discussed, but the Society was allowed to resume in 1821, provided that no political matters of the past 20 years were debated.

Foster's, the second bank to be established, opened in 1813 at 55 Bridge Street, moving in 1836 to the Elizabethan building, now the Turk's Head Restaurant, in Trinity Street. The Cambridge Philosophical Society was founded in 1819 mainly by Henslow and Adam Sedgwick. Henslow introduced practical work in botany, and influenced the youthful Charles Darwin, and Sedgwick lectured regularly on geology and built up a fine collection of specimens.

In 1812, undergraduates who appeared in Hall in trousers were considered absent because breeches and gaiters were the correct wear, and boots were forbidden. Trousers did not begin to be worn until about 1824.

*   *   *

No additional colleges had been founded since the end of the seventeenth century, but when Sir George Downing died in 1749, he left money for a new college. Legal difficulties delayed the completion of the first buildings, designed by William Wilkins, until 1812. In 1796 the Corporation offered two sites, Pound Hill or Parker's Piece. Had the latter been chosen, the city would have lost one of the finest public open spaces possessed by any town.

An island site called Doll's Close in Maid's Causeway was actually bought from the town in 1810 for £350, but abandoned in favour of Pembroke Leys, formerly Swinecroft. This ground was purchased from ten owners, and compensation had to paid to over 200 householders who lost pasture rights. It provided a site upon which the college buildings could be placed around a spacious lawn, and was in fact so large that a considerable area was later sold to the university for many buildings, mostly for branches of science.

In the meantime, the site extended to the south side of Downing Street, and there was a proposal for a new road to run in a straight line from the end of Jesus Lane, along the east side of the Market Place and Corn Exchange Street to St Andrew's Hill, with the new college making an impressive termination to a long vista, but the scheme was not adopted.

*   *   *

A notice displayed in 1822 stated that 'Zachariah Whitmore of Philadelphia, N. America, begs to inform the inhabitants of Cambridge that he intends starting from Lynn on his Water Velocipede at 12 o'clock, and will arrive at Cambridge between 6 and 7 o'clock in the evening on Whit Monday next.' About 2,000 people waited for several hours, and finally discovered that they had been hoaxed.

*   *   *

Visitors who came from London in 1820 saw the first houses at the corner of Lensfield Road. On the left, a wall enclosing the grounds of Mr Pemberton extended to the end of what is now St Peter's Terrace. The wall ran almost along the centre of the present road, making Trumpington Street very narrow. From here to Peterhouse was a row of about 25 small houses and shops, which were demolished after 1821 to form part of the site of the Fitzwilliam Museum. Peterhouse was obscured by a high wall, then came two inns, the Half Moon and the Cardinal's Cap, both among many houses.

Corpus had not yet built its Front Court, designed by Wilkins; this was begun in 1823. King's Parade was very narrow, with shops and houses on both sides, until 1823, when the tenants on the college side were given notice to quit, and the buildings were replaced by Wilkins' Screen. At the entrance to Trinity Street, shops and houses still occupied the site of Waterhouse's Caius building. Rose Crescent did not yet exist; this curved terrace occupying the former yard of the Rose Inn was not built until 1826.

Green Street had just become a thoroughfare for vehicles; until 1819 the Sidney Street end had been blocked by two houses, leaving only a narrow passage for pedestrians. St John's still had its old Chapel, and the Round Church was surrounded by a wall about 18 feet high.

Ackerman (1815) says of Emmanuel: 'This college is pleasantly situated at the south-eastern extremity of the town, commanding a large extent of open country, bounded by the Gog Magog hills.'

Until 1818 there were no houses surrounding Parker's Piece, and the first was built on Parkside by Charles Humfrey, a banker. He owned the ground between Melbourne Place and Christ's Pieces, and built several streets of houses, including a large one for himself. Houses built in Orchard Street for his servants had no windows on one side so that he would not be overlooked.

In about 1820 residents of Market Street sent a petition to the Council, complaining that their peace and comfort were destroyed on Saturdays by the crowds which assembled to hear ballads sung. They prayed that measures might be taken so that 'the ears of respectable inhabitants may not be assailed by the disgusting obscenities which are often uttered.'

The Corporation exacted a toll of 2d on all loaded carts entering or

eaving the town. These tolls caused much resentment and in 1824 some
inhabitants raised a fund to challenge the Corporation in the courts. Three
of the principal firms refused to pay tolls, the Corporation took legal
action, and a verdict in favour of the defendants deprived the
Corporation of half its income.

John Grafton, one of the pioneers of the gas industry, came to live in
Maid's Causeway in about 1820, and by 1823 some of the streets were
lit by 'oil gas.' A little later, Grafton began to make coal gas in retorts at
Gas Lane, near St Matthew's Street. He contracted to light the streets
with inflammable gas obtained from coal, and transferred his plant to
River Lane, where coal coming by lighters from King's Lynn could be
unloaded. The Cambridge Gas-Light Company took over Grafton's plant
and contracts in 1834, and three years later the company obtained
additional powers and changed its name to The Cambridge University
and Town Gas Light Co. A rival company appeared, but ran into
difficulties and was acquired by the old.

In 1833 'Mr. Farraday and a number of scientific gentlemen visited
the National Gallery of Practical Science (London) to see the first
exhibition of Hick's Patent Cooking by gas. Several pigeons were roasted
and a piece of mutton boiled and served up to the numerous spectators at
which the ladies particularly expressed themselves delighted. The
advantage of this mode is economy and certainty.'

George Pryme, who laid the foundations of economic studies in
Cambridge, was the first professor of political economy at any British
university. He was one of the first dons to take an active interest in town
affairs, and became known as 'Counsellor Pryme.' He was M.P. for the
town for several years, and addressed a letter to the freemen and
inhabitants of Cambridge in which he said that 'The manner in which 35
years ago, you were bartered and conveyed away, like the slaves on a
Russian estate, or a West Indian plantation, is well known to you all.'

In his *Autobiographical Recollections* he mentions parliamentary
elections: 'I can remember Lord Godolphin and Mr. Adeane being borne
down St. Andrew's Street sitting on wooden chairs fastened to poles, and
supported on men's shoulders. The chairs were covered with party colours
and, every now and then, the procession would stop and the chairs tossed
up as high as the bearers could reach.

*　　　*　　　*

In 1811 there were only about 800 undergraduates in residence, but afte
1819 there were more students at Cambridge than at Oxford, and severa
colleges were enlarged between then and 1830. Some of the students had
to lodge in the town, and in 1818 the university established a system fo
licensing lodging-house keepers. George Pryme, writing of Trinity, say
that 'in 1823 the first stone was laid of a new court on ground occupied
by the dwelling-house of the baker and cook and a large baking-office'
where all the college bread was baked.' Originally called King's Court
and later New Court, it was designed in a neo-Gothic style by Wilkins
the most important collegiate architect of his time. Pryme also says tha
'When partly built it was burnt out, and the £40,000 left to complete i
was mostly spent on repairs. It was, therefore, finished off shabbily, with
stucco instead of stone, except the river front.'

Wilkins also designed the New Court of Corpus in 1823-7, and he
considered it to be his best work in the Gothic style. He won a
competition for new buildings for King's, and built the range which
includes the Hall, Library, and former Provost's Lodge. Wilkins
proposed that Gibb's Fellows' Building should be Gothicised, but
fortunately lack of money prevented this. His Screen facing King's
Parade displaced a fine grove of trees behind the demolished shops and
houses; members of the college had sometimes been allowed to shoot the
rooks which built in them.

St John's New Court was begun in 1827, partially occupied in 1830,
and when it was completed in 1831 it was then the largest single building
of any college. The swampy nature of the site necessitated the removal of
the peaty subsoil, and a vast quantity of timber was placed on the
underlying gravel, then a large mass of brickwork with vaulted cellars
£65,000 of the total cost of £78,000 had to be borrowed, and the debt
was not cleared until 1857.

In the early part of the nineteenth century the government of the
university was to a large extent in the hands of the Masters, and they
behaved like Grand Dukes, associating only with one another. When a
man became Master of his college, he would often behave coldly and
autocratically to Fellows who had been old and intimate friends. When
he gave a dinner party, only other Masters and their wives were invited.
At a dinner given by Dr Corrie, Master of Jesus, one of the guests was H.
A. Morgan, a Tutor. Three Masters present so resented that he had joined

their select company that they did not speak to him throughout the evening.

Dr Mansel of Trinity, however, began to give evening parties, sometimes with music and dancing, probably because he had six unmarried daughters whom he desired to present to society. Mr Serjeant Frere, who had lived for many years in London, became Master of Downing, and to the horror of the other Masters, refused to accept their narrow exclusiveness. An accomplished singer, he gave musical parties and *tableaux vivants* in the Lodge, and plays were performed in the Hall. At one of these parties, to which Masters and their wives had been invited, other guests arrived later. A Master's wife afterwards remarked, 'Some people came in the evening, of course we went away.'

Even in church a strict order of precedence had to be observed. In Great St Mary's, seats were labelled 'For the wives of Professors,' 'For the Wives of Doctors of Divinity', etc.

'Socius,' in *Facetiae Cantabrigiensis* (1825) says that breakfast-parties were generally considered the most popular form of entertainment, patronized by reading and non-reading men, and the Simeonites. 'Served at 11 o'clock, there is no lack of entertainment; toast and muffins, ham and tongue, ducks and fowls, sausages and beefsteaks, red herrings and anchovies, pigeon and veal pies, snipes and widgeon, etc. etc., hot and cold, vie with one another in amiable profusion; for drinkables: chocolate, coffee, cocoa, tea, ale, porter, soda-water, and, sometimes, various wines.'

A Classical Tripos was instituted in 1822. Educated persons studied the Greek and Latin authors, and classical allusions constantly appeared in speeches, conversation, and correspondence. A man was not regarded as well-educated if he could not quote or recognise passages from Virgil, Ovid, Cicero, Horace, or Seneca.

In 1829 the university purchased the old court of King's and there were ambitious plans to demolish the existing buildings and erect a quadrangle as an extension to the University Library. Only one range was built, in 1836-42, and the architect, Cockerell, successfully combined Roman styles with his own innovations. Had the complete court been built, it would have been one of the most important neo-classical works of the period. The town erected a new gaol, with 50 cells, in Gonville Place, in a castellated style, having an archway in imitation of a portcullis between two massive towers. 'The chief occupation of prisoners is the tread-wheel labour for pumping water, oakum-picking, making mats and clothing, etc,' says a contemporary guidebook.

The Shakespeare Club, founded in 1830, gave quarterly performances in the Hoop Hotel, and three years later some seceding members founded the Garrick Club. An Act of 1844, not repealed until 1894, prohibited any theatre within 14 miles of Cambridge. The Botanic Garden had become too small and too near the centre of the town, and in 1831 the university purchased from Trinity Hall 50 acres of cornfields beside the Trumpington Road. An old gravel pit was transformed into a lake, glasshouses were constructed, and by the 70's the garden was well established with a collection of trees and plants second only to Kew.

The Pitt Building of the University Press was erected in 1831-32 with funds subscribed to provide a national monument to William Pitt, who in 1783 had become the country's youngest Prime Minister. When statues had been put up in Hanover Square and Westminster Abbey, a handsome sum of money remained, and Dr Monk, Bishop of Gloucester, suggested that it might be used to enlarge the Press, which was almost opposite Pembroke where Pitt had been a scholar. The architect was Edward Blore, who had built Abbotsford for Sir Walter Scott. At first the Press used only the wings of the building, and the remainder became a temporary store for the paintings and drawings intended for the Fitzwilliam Museum. From 1836-1934, the University Registrary was housed there.

A building for the study of anatomy was erected in 1833 at the corner of Downing Street and Corn Exchange Street, and on the evening of 2 December it was attacked by a mob who erroneously believed that the body of a pauper was being dissected in contravention of the Anatomy Act. The Riot Act had to be read and the building was considerably damaged before the attack was repulsed, largely with the assistance of undergraduates. Heavy iron bars were later installed to protect doors and windows. This building was demolished in 1891.

*   *   *

In 1829 Charles Humfrey made *A Report on the Present State of the River Cam,* with some suggestions for the improvement of the navigation. The average depth was only three feet, and during times of drought the barges, which had to be restricted to a draught of two feet eight inches and a load of 20 tons, sometimes took four days to travel from Clayhithe to Cambridge. As a result of this report, the river was deepened, locks at the Pike and Eel and Clayhithe eliminated, and the Jesus Green lock rebuilt

Garret Hostel Bridge was repaired in 1832, but a handbill circulated in 1833 by the Deputy Town Clerk said that 'Notice is hereby given, that the bridge called or known by the name of Gerard Hostel Bridge, at the end of Trinity College back lane, is now unsafe for the passage of horses; the public are therefore informed that the said bridge will be stopped up against the passage of horses, until the same can be repaired.'

The works undertaken after Humfrey's Report had made the river seven feet deep in the centre, but much shallower near the banks. Stuart wrote: 'In rowing at Cambridge we used to be very much troubled by the weeds which infested the river at certain seasons of the year and which caught our oars. Sometimes it was so thick that the boats could scarcely pass through it.' The offending weed, *Anacharis Alsinastrum,* commonly called the Canadian Water Weed, had found its way accidentally to this country, being first noticed in Berwickshire in 1842.

In 1847 a specimen was planted in a tub at the Botanic Garden, and in the following year the Curator placed a piece in the Conduit Stream. Within a year the weed had spread all along this stream, passed through a pipe beneath Trumpington Road into Vicar's Brook, and then into the river. By 1852, i.e. in four years, the one small piece had multiplied so vigorously that it impeded navigation and drainage throughout many miles of the river. Boats were unable to enter or leave the railway docks at Ely, watermen complained that at the Backs of the Colleges additional horses had to be used to pull barges, and rowing, swimming, and fishing became difficult. Although this plant thrived so well far from its native habitat, a visiting American professor said that it did not spread in his own country.

On 30 September 1848, the *Cambridge Chronicle* reported that 'On Wednesday evening the sloop *Mary Ann,* a small sea-going vessel of about 30 tons burden, arrived at Cambridge with a cargo of coals. With the exception of the steamer that plied to Lynn some years ago, we believe that this is the only sea-going vessel that has come up to Cambridge within living memory, and, of course, she created no little

sensation as she came up the river with her (comparatively) large set sail.'
And, on 3 October: 'The dredging of the river Cam . . . has begun and,
when finished, the success of the recent voyage of the *Mary Ann* will
induce others to navigate still larger vessels, which will be a greater
advantage to the town and neighbourhood in the shape of a diminution in
the price of coals.'

The River Cam Navigation Act of 1851 placed the river between
King's Mill and Clayhithe under the care of 11 conservators; five
representing the county, three the university, and three the town council.

Until the middle of the nineteenth century, only King's, Trinity, and St
John's had musical services in their chapels. They shared one organist and
six lay clerks, mostly elderly, who had to hurry from place to place.

From the early days of the university there were frequent complaints
about the dress of the students. Dr Whewell, writing in 1837 when he
was a Fellow and tutor of Trinity, says 'It may be, too, that with an
improvement in many respects, there is an increased laxity in the
observance of rules on other points; for example, the constant use of
academic dress. But in most such cases, the fault is in those of superior
position, who ought to force the observance of rules, and who are not
sufficiently vigilant and earnest in this part of their duty. *Nos, nos consules
desumus.* If, for instance, all persons in the Universities, who have pupils
under their care, were persuaded that the academic dress is a valuable
remembrance of the duties and obligations of the student's position, and
were to enjoin its use on all occasions, and to rebuke its absence, there can
be little doubt that omission in this respect might soon be rendered as rare
as it ever was.'

EIGHT

University Sport, Municipal Reform

Until about 1825, few students played cricket, football, or rowed. Those who could not afford to ride gained their exercise by walking to Grantchester or Coton, and on wet days the wide cloisters of Nevile's Court at Trinity were thronged with men pacing up and down. Simeon advised his students that every day they should make sure that the third milestone from Cambridge was still in its place.

At Eton there are lists of Captains of Boats going back to 1812, and Westminster School had a six-oar in 1813. C. F. R. Bayley, who came into residence at Cambridge in October 1823, stated that there were then available for hire two 6-oars, three or four 4-oars, and many smaller boats. In the Spring of 1825, Bayley and three others from Trinity hired a four-oar called *Shannon* in which they rowed regularly, easily beating any scratch crews that they met.

St John's formed a Boat Club in 1825 and Dean Merivale said that their boat was 'of prodigious strength and weight, standing high in the water . . . like a three-decker,' and that it carried a 'Tin Panthermanticon' containing two kettles, nine plates, four dishes, a canvas table, a charcoal bag, and a phosphorous bottle, etc. The first eight-oar boat on the Cam was manned by Johnians.

In 1826 a Trinity ten-oar boat, built in London, proved to be superior when the rivals met. The steerer of the Johnian boat occasionally blew a bugle to indicate its position to the Trinity boat, which gave chase and usually succeeded in bumping the stern of its rival. In 1827, one 10-oar, two or three eight-oar, and a six-oar belonging to Caius began regular bumping-races. In 1828 and 1829 there were eight or ten racing boats

holding contests three times a week in all three terms, and for three years
the Trinity boat was only beaten once.

Boat races had begun earlier at Oxford, where the river was deeper
and wider. In 1829 a challenge was sent to Oxford, and it was agreed
that a race would be held at Henley on a course of about two miles. The
Oxford crew proved to be stronger and more skilful, and in this first race
the Oxford men wore dark blue striped jerseys and the Cambridge men
pink sashes. In 1836 the Cambridge crew were in white, but just before
the race a Christ's man bought some light blue ribbon to fasten to the
bows.

Most of the undergraduates who played cricket came from a few great
schools, Eton supplying a large proportion. Westminster and Eton began
to play matches in the middle of the eighteenth century, and a newspaper
report of 1788 says that 'Cambridge Old Etonians have for 30 years
played the Rest of the University upon Parker's Piece.' The University
Cricket Club was probably founded by three Etonians in 1824-5, their
first ground an enclosed field of eight acres off Mill Road. At the first
Oxford and Cambridge match in 1827, the players wore knee breeches,
silk stockings, and had neither pads nor gloves.

From 1846 the club moved to two fields divided by a ditch in
Gresham Road, rented by F. P. Fenner, who for long had been an
outstanding batsman of the Town XI. W. C. Deacon, captain in 1850,
said that the ground was so rough that he was once knocked senseless by
a ball. In 1861 Fenner appointed Watts custodian and he remained there
until 1908. He planted 150 trees and in 1864 constructed the
cinder-track. During his early years, trespassers invaded the ground and
climbed trees to see a man being hanged at the adjacent gaol.

The ground was sold to the university club in 1894. A net was
reserved for the Prince of Wales, and a pitch made for him at Madingley
Hall. This was very rough and it was said that the Prince was very plucky
in standing up to the bowling. When the county side met the then
pre-eminent Surrey team at Fenner's in 1861, the Prince gave £5
towards the expenses.

Among the university players, Prince Ranjitsinhji, commonly known as
Ranji, was outstanding. He was the most attractive personality and the
most amazing batsman of his time, and crowds flocked to matches when
he was playing, as they had flocked to see Dr Grace. One contemporary

said 'He's no cricketer. He's a conjurer, an Eastern juggler.'

The university cricketers were coached by a number of outstanding town players. Cambridgeshire is no longer among the leading cricketing counties, but in the 1880's, no other county had a pair of batsmen to equal Tom Hayward, uncle of the great Surrey cricketer, and Robert Carpenter, the best exponent of back-play of his time. William (Billy) Buttress was one of the greatest break bowlers of all time, the man most dreaded by contemporary batsmen, and W. G. Grace said that George Tarrant was the fastest bowler he had faced. When the All-England XI was in its prime, it contained four Cambridge players; three were chosen to tour America in 1859, and three to go to Australia in 1863-4.

For many years, before they acquired their own grounds, college teams played on Parker's Piece, and at times there were so many games in progress that fielders became intermingled. Some colleges pooled their resources to secure the Amalgamation Ground. Parker's Piece had come into the possession of the town in 1613, but until 1831 it remained rough and marshy, divided by a ditch and a hedge. Mr Dupuis of King's then sought and gained permission to level about 60 square yards 'in order to afford greater facility for playing the manly game of cricket'.

More levelling was carried out in 1839, 1845, and 1860, and in 1862 a public notice said that 'The Commons Committee have received many complaints of the injury done to Parker's Piece by horsemen exercising over every part of the same. The Committee have no wish to interfere with the recreation of the inhabitants, but they must request that gentlemen will not exercise their horses on the Piece, except within 25 yards of the railings, and that they will give particular directions to their servants on all occasions to comply with this regulation.'

G. E. Corrie, Master of Jesus, wrote on 10 December 1838, that 'In walking with Willis we passed by Parker's Piece and there saw some 40 gownsmen playing at football. The novelty and liveliness of the scene was very amusing.' One may claim that Cambridge is the birthplace of association football. Students who played on the Piece in the middle of the ninteenth century came from schools with varying conceptions of the rules. As W. G. Green wrote in *Memories of Eton and King's, 1851-58,* 'There was a Football Club, whose games were played on Parker's Piece according to rules more like the Eton Field rules than any other. But Rugby and Harrow players would sometimes begin running with the ball in hand or claiming free kicks, which led to some protest and confusion.'

'A Trinity man, Beamont (a Fellow of his college soon after) was a regular attendant, and the rules were revised by him and one or two others, with concessions to non-Etonians. Few from King's College ever played at this University game, and about the end of my time there began to be other special Rugby games on another ground.'

Henry Jackson wrote: 'When I went to Cambridge in 1858, old Rugbeans had a game once or twice in the season in memory of the past; but the notion was that football was a game for boys. Then the Harrow men and the Eton men started their respective games. Then they began to learn one another's games. Then 'association' was deliberately invented. We had no definite notion of passing when I played the Rugby game.'

In 1848, representatives from various schools met to formulate rules in order to obtain uniformity, and affixed them to trees on Parker's Piece. In later life, when many of the young men had become schoolmasters or clergymen, they taught these rules throughout the country. Rules were again discussed in 1862, and when the Football Association was formed in 1863, the Cambridge rules were adopted almost completely, and were later accepted throughout the world.

In the early days, the captains attempted to ensure that their teams obeyed the rules. Later, each side had its own umpire, who, carrying a stick, patrolled his own team's half. When an infringement occurred, an umpire raised his stick and play was stopped to allow the umpires to confer. When they could not agree, they referred the matter to a third person sitting on a chair at the halfway line, and he became known as the referee. In 1890 it was decided to abolish the umpires and to allow the referee on to the field to control the game.

The University Swimming Club was founded in 1855. Ground beside the river was acquired at Newnham, and a fund was raised to erect a long wooden shed to accommodate about 120 bathers. The first inter-varsity match was held at the Crown Baths, Kensington Oval, in 1891. Oscar Browning was secretary, and G. Lowes Dickinson says that 'his corpulent person was constantly to be found in the state of primitive nudity which, in those early and happy days, was characteristic of Cambridge bathing. For even in the meadows open to view, where the members of the town bathed, they ran quite naked in crowds over the green grass'.

No modest female approached the town bathing place on Sheep's Green and Coe Fen, and ladies who passed in boats opened parasols so that they might not see the naked men and boys. In 1894 a ladder was provided above the iron bridge for the use of female bathers, and as this adjoined the men's bathing place, there were many letters in the press supporting or opposing the custom of nude bathing for men and boys. In 1896 an enclosure for women was provided, and Miss Hardy became custodian at a salary of ten shillings a week.

Charles Bristed, in *Five Years in an English University* (1852) says that 'There is not so much riding as might be supposed . . . The expense is the reason generally alleged . . . There is sufficient business, however, for 5 or 6 livery stables, those who keep their own horses being mostly the Noblemen and Fellow-Commoners and a few of the Fellows.' And L. Austen Leigh says: 'I remember Green Street so full of polo ponies you couldn't walk down it.'

Ralph Nevill, in *Unconventional Memories,* says of Magdalene, which he entered in 1856, 'The college then easy-going to an extreme; besides being permeated with a sporting set, quite a number belonged to families which for generations had been identified with sport. Many kept hunters and polo ponies, and one a coach (kept some distance out of the town) and drove four in hand to Newmarket when racing was going on there.'

Until the 1870's, students were not allowed to visit billiard rooms, although for many years the prohibition had been violated. The *History Gazetteer and Directory of Cambridgeshire, etc.* 1851, stated that 'There are also several billiard establishments here, of which the most commodious and extensive are those of Mr. John Brown in Parker's-street and the Ram-yard, Bridge Street.'

John Brown had an eventful life which he described in *Sixty Years' Gleanings from Life's Harvest* (1858). He was born in 1796, apprenticed to a shoemaker, and later served in the army. He deserted from the army, acted for a strolling company, went to sea, and returned to London to become a skilled shoemaker. In 1831 he returned to Cambridge and had several public-houses until he set up again as a shoemaker. His shop was burgled, he was made bankrupt and imprisoned. Having some knowledge of billiards, he bought a wooden table and taught the game to his fellow townsmen. This latest venture proved to be profitable, and he was able to have a second billiard-room built, bought another table and converted it into a slate table.

A notice in the window, 'Billiards, a Slate Table' attracted university custom and he purchased a new table from Burroughes & Watts. 'My tables, rooms, and appointments were acknowledged to be the best in the town,' and he claimed that hundreds of the best gentlemen players throughout the world had graduated at his establishment. After four years, a university official attempted to enforce the statute prohibiting billiards. Brown installed bells and whistles to give notice of the man's approach, whereupon the gaslights were extinguished and students escaped through a window. Eventually he was summoned to appear before a university court, but he obtained permission to carry on.

He had a coach-house and stabling built, and let out horses and vehicles. When the railway opened in 1845, journeys were expensive, so Brown formed a company to run a four-horse coach to London, but this ceased after six months because his employees had stolen about £800. Having now 'the largest establishment of the kind in the provinces, and second only to one in London,' he became a member of the Town Council and wore a silk gown trimmed with sable. There were several rival billiard rooms, but Brown enlarged his premises and finally had two public rooms for pool and billiards, seven private billiard rooms, and a racket-court. The best public room was 30 feet by 20 feet with skylights and chandeliers. Towards the end of his career, John Brown was looked upon as an institution in the town, and almost as important as a college tutor.

*   *   *

Under the Reform Act of 1832, £10 householders were entitled to vote and freemen who lived more than seven miles from the town were disfranchised. This increased the number of voters to 1,247.

The Municipal Corporations Commission began investigations in Cambridge in 1833, and a leading article in The *Times* said that 'Probably no judicial investigation into a public trust ever brought to light more shameless profligacy or more inveterate dishonesty, more bare-faced venality in politics, a more heartless disregard of the claims of the poor in the perversion of the funds left for their benefit, or a more degrading subserviency to the views of the rich when they appeared in the shape of patrons or distributors of places, a more insatiable cupidity in the corporate officers to enrich themselves with the corporate property, or a more entire neglect of their duties and functions as magistrates, than are presented by the evidence now before us.'

The affairs of a population of over 20,000 had been controlled by 158 freemen of whom only 118 resided in the town. These men and their friends had acquired Corporation property at much below its true value. Alderman Butcher, solicitor to Mortlock, had obtained the lease of both sides of Regent Street for £30, a total frontage of 1,386 feet worth 24s. a foot in 1810. He had also acquired a frontage of 345 feet in Maid's Causeway for two guineas, which he sold soon after for £345.

Another alderman had paid a guinea for land worth £150; a third paid £40 for two acres in Hills Road and sold them a year later for £400. Property in Bridge Street, leased on fines of about £200 at a rent of £23, was improved by the erection of a small summer-house and then sold for £3,750. It is not surprising that the Corporation was described as being 'uniformly hostile and indifferent to the interests of the town at large.'

A common Councilman told the Commission that 'As it was only Corporation property I would not make the same calculation for a stranger as for a friend. I would make a little difference, and sometimes a great difference, in favour of a friend – because it was only Corporation property.'

In the previous 14 years, the Corporation had spent £480 from public funds for public purposes, and £1,300 on dinners. The quays were in bad repair and the bridges unsafe. Many streets were still unpaved, and while the university contributed about £1,200 a year for paving and lighting the streets, the Corporation contributed ony £10. Mire on Coe Fen came up to horses' knees, and medical men considered that unless it were drained it would be fatal to the health of the town. It was drained by public subscription at a cost of £150, the Corporation 'liberally' contributing £10.

The police were inefficient, and the chief and high constables, the 51 constables and six watchmen did less to keep order than the proctors and their servants. The condition of the town during Long Vacations was scandalous. Professor Sedgwick told the Commissioners that when he was Senior Proctor, police duties during term fell exclusively on himself and his colleagues, that he received no assistance from the magistrates, and, generally speaking, never saw any indication of a street police.

At a public meeting held in 1834 it was decided that a regular police force should be established, but the scheme was abandoned because of the impending reform of municipal corporations. The Municipal Corporations Act reduced the number of aldermen to ten and increased the councillors to 30, to be elected by the ratepayers. At the first election, all of the aldermen who stood for re-election were defeated. In 1836 the Town Council established a police force consisting of a Superintendent, two Inspectors, four Sergeants, and 24 Constables.

In 1834, 300 electors dined at the Hoop Hotel to celebrate the re-election of the Rt Hon. Thomas Spring Rice to Parliament, and in the same year the Shakespeare Club erected a new portable stage and scenery in the large room. W. Bird opened the University Arms Hotel and announced 'to the nobility and gentry of the university, town and county of Cambridge that he has entered upon the above hotel and posting house, every window of which commands extensive and pleasing views . . . and affords a most airy and salubrious retreat for valetudinarians or families visiting Cambridge.'

*   *   *

A description of the installation of the Marquis Camden as Chancellor in 1835 will give some indication of the lavish round of garden-parties, balls and dinners which were normal on such occasions. His arrival on Saturday was heralded by the ringing of bells and salvos of shot. A university procession accompanied him to Trinity, and in the evening a masque was performed at Downing. On Sunday morning there was a service in Great St Mary's, and among those present were Prince George of Cambridge, numerous dukes, earls, marquises and knights, the Archbishop of Canterbury and three bishops. The company then heard an anthem in King's College Chapel.

On Monday a troop of yeomanry met the Duke of Wellington, who was to receive an Honorary Degree. In the Senate House, the Chancellor was installed, supported by Prince George and the Duke of Cumberland, and Honorary Degrees were conferred. In the afternoon there was an entertainment in the grounds of Sidney, followed by a banquet at Jesus which lasted for four hours. On Tuesday morning, in the Senate House,

Opposite: Petty Cury, from J. J. Smith's **The Cambridge Portfolio,** *1840*

here was music, more Honorary Degrees were conferred, and a number
of scholars discoursed in prose and verse in Greek and Latin. Finally the
nstallation Ode was sung. Guests then attended a banquet at Caius, and
another feast at Trinity.

On Wednesday the principal guests visited the University Press, then
went to a gala in the grounds of Downing, and to dinner in a large
marquee erected in the New Court of St John's, followed by a ball in the
Guildhall. On Thursday a banquet beginning at 5 o'clock was given in
Nevile's Court, which was gay with flags and flowers. There were tents
on the lawns, bands of music, and tables groaning with food and wines.
This was followed by a dinner at King's which possibly outrivalled in
magnificence all of the preceding entertainments. In the meantime, Trinity
was still thronged with dancers, and at midnight there was a firework
display, and a convoy of eights came up the river.

For the banquet at Jesus, it had been thought that the Hall would not
hold all the guests, so a canvas roof had been erected over a court and the
ground boarded. On the preceding evening there was heavy rain, and the
canvas roof was found to be far from waterproof. In the event, it was
found after all that the Hall would suffice.

*   *   *

. H. Case, who joined King's College choir in 1836, says that the boys
had free schooling, the schoolmaster being also the butler of Clare, and
dinners of bread and meat and half a pint of small beer. There were
puddings only on two feast days in the year. The boys were paid 6s. 4d
or two quarters, and 2s. 6d for the other two quarters. The six senior
boys were provided with a swallowtail coat.

King's obtained its Fellows' Garden when St Giles' parish was
inclosed. In 1836 the field nearest to the road was fenced and used for
the Provost's four coach-horses. It was not laid out as a pleasure garden
until 1851. In 1837, ten coaches left Cambridge for London every
weekday, and many more went to other towns. Among them were the
Norfolk Regulator, the Fakenham Hero, the Wisbech Defiance, the Bee
Hive, the Rising Sun, Blucher, Tally Ho, the Telegraph, and the Rocket.

The seventh Viscount Fitzwilliam left to the university the interest on
£100,000 and his important collection of pictures, engravings,

Opposite top: *Annual Examination in Trinity College, by R. W. Buss, 1842*
Opposite bottom: *The Cloisters and Library in Nevile's Court, Trinity College, by
and H. S. Storer, 1842*

illuminated manuscripts and books, including paintings by Titian
Rembrandt, and Veronese. The Fitzwilliam Museum, designed b
George Basevi, was begun in 1837. Sites previously considered were th
Bull Hotel; King's Parade in front of the college; Senate House Yard
between Great St Mary's and St Michael's church; or on the opposit
side of Trinity Street now occupied by the Waterhouse building of Caius

After the death of Basevi in 1845, C. R. Cockerell designed th
impressive entrance hall, then lack of funds caused work to be suspended
and the building was completed by E. M. Barry in 1870-5. There hav
since been several additions. Further along Trumpington Stree
Peterhouse was still masked by a wall and a writer of 1840 said: 'It is t
be regretted that the College does not present to the street somethin
better than a brick wall. In this iron age they might at least substitute
handsome palisade or stockade of that material.'

The staff of the University Library consisted of a librarian and tw
assistants. Undergraduates were not admitted, and even B.A.s were no
allowed to borrow books until 1829. The University Sermons, whic
took place at 2 p.m. on Sundays during term, were important occasions
University and Mayoral processions went to a church crowded with me
in gowns of black, blue, scarlet, silver or gold, and ladies in their be
dresses and ornate hats. In the evening, hundreds of people who had bee
present would discuss the sermon, the manner in which it had bee
delivered, and the subject.

Trinity College Chapel, on a Sunday evening, presented a strikin
sight, the Master with Noblemen seated on his right, the Fellows in th
upper seats, the choir in the centre, and hundreds of junior members i
other parts of the Chapel, all in white surplices. Students from othe
colleges, after their own services, came to the antechapel to listen to th
organ. Many people thought that at the daily services at Trinity, th
presence of the markers, men who walked up and down during
considerable part of the service with lists, running a pin through the name
of those present, was incongruous and disturbing.

*   *   *

The celebrations in Cambridge for the Coronation of Queen Victori
in 1838 were more extensive than any seen before. In the centre c
Parker's Piece, staging was erected for 100 musicians and vocalist:

surrounded by a rotunda for 1,600 spectators and a circular enclosure for another 6,000 persons. Around this were three rows of tables for nearly 3,000 children. From these circles, 60 tables, each 125 feet long, radiated like the spokes of a wheel, and these were enclosed by an outer ring of 28 tables and a roped-off space for 6,000 more spectators.

15,000 persons sat down to a meal of 7,029 joints of meat, 4,500 loaves of bread, 1,608 plum puddings, and 99 barrels of ale, with large quantities of mustard, salt, pickles, tobacco, and snuff. Men were allowed three pints of ale, women one pint, and children half a pint. There was a balloon ascent, and at night a grand display of fireworks superintended by Mr Deck, a local chemist, 'whose displays, as an amateur in the pyrotechnic art, have upon former occasions elicited so much well-merited admiration'.

Balloon ascents were a popular diversion, thus on 13 May 1831, 'By permission of the Right-Worshipful the Vice-Chancellor, and the worshipful Mayor of Cambridge, Mr. Green, junr. begs to announce to the Nobility and Gentry of the University, Town and County of Cambridge, that he proposes making his 59th aerial voyage on Monday next at five o'clock, from a spacious and commodious enclosure in High Street, Barnwell. Sheltered seats will be provided for ladies. A band of music will be in attendance. Should the day prove calm it is Mr. Green's intention to make partial ascents. Admission – two shillings each – children and servants half-price.'

A year later, 'Mr Green, junr., took his 70th aerial trip from Mr. Warwicker's premises at Barnwell. The descent was made with perfect safety near the village of Foulmire, but the travellers had a somewhat unusual, and it is thought extravagant, call made upon them by one of the farmers for damage done to his corn, and to whom £7 was ultimately paid.'

The examinations for mathematical honours were held in the Old Schools until 1839, then in lecture-rooms of Trinity. Held in January, they lasted for six days, and there was always great excitement when results were announced in the Senate House. The other examinations were held there, and to prevent anyone from helping a neighbour, there were two sets of examination papers, distributed so that no contiguous men had the same paper. Colleges also held annual examinations at the end of May or the beginning of June.

Queen Victoria and Prince Albert visited Cambridge in November, 1843. They were met at Royston by over 3,000 yeomanry commanded by Lord Hardwicke and they 'swept over hedges and ditches, so that by the time they reached Cambridge, every man was a pillar of mud, and every horse a mass of living vapour.' They were met by the Mayor and Council in Trumpington Street, where a magnificent triumphal arch resembling Temple Bar and festooned with flowers and laurels spanned the street.

The Queen's carriage drove into Trinity Great Court, where over 2,000 members of the university waited, and she was presented with the college keys, 'large, ponderous and rusty, strapped together by an old greasy bit of leather'. Addresses were presented in the Hall, where a throne had been erected, and the royal pair attended evening service in King's College Chapel. It had been intended that they would then visit Trinity Library, but the Queen asked to see the Chapel and Newton's statue instead. The red carpet leading to the Hall was hurriedly removed to lead towards the Chapel, but was found to be too short, so undergraduates, in the spirit of Sir Walter Raleigh, flung down their gowns.

After dinner in the Lodge there was a splendid levée, the town was illuminated and there was a firework display on Parker's Piece. It is recorded that the Queen slept soundly in a bed adorned with 'what was once a praying-carpet of a great Mandarin, and was snatched from the fingers of his wife at the storming of Ningpo.' On the following day, the Queen went to the Senate House, where an Honorary Degree was given to the Prince Consort. They visited several colleges, and later left for the country seat, Wimpole Hall, of Lord Hardwicke.

*   *   *

In 1842 the massive gatehouse of the Castle was demolished, and a new Shire House erected; a Corn Exchange was built at the junction of Downing Street and Corn Exchange Street, and an iron bridge was erected at Silver Street, replacing a timber bridge, at a cost of nearly £2,000; over £700 came from subscriptions. A Free Library was established in 1845 in the Friends' Meeting-House, and remained there until 1862.

The first train arrived in Cambridge on 29 July 1845. It had 13 double carriages and one open carriage bringing the band of the Coldstream Guards, and a celebration dinner, attended by the Mayor and Corporation and railway officials, was held in tents erected outside the station. In 1836 there had been a proposal for a line from London to York, passing through Cambridge and with a station on Jesus Green, but this was abandoned. In the same year, a Bill sanctioned a line with a station in what is now Latham Road.

Shortage of capital prevented the company from getting beyond Bishop's Stortford, but the line eventually reached Cambridge in 1845, the station being placed far from the centre of the town at the insistence of the university. An Act of 1844 empowered the university to supervise the movements of students. Proctors and other officials could enter stations when trains were due, could demand information about students travelling or intending to travel, and could require the company to refuse to carry a student, even if he had paid his fare.

The company was required to employ special constables under university control, and it was prohibited from taking up or setting down any person at Cambridge, or within three miles of Cambridge, between 10 a.m. and 3 p.m. on Sundays, with a penalty of £5 per person. In 1851, the Vice-Chancellor protested about Sunday excursions to Cambridge, saying in a letter to the directors that 'he expressed his pain that they had made arrangements for conveying foreigners and others to Cambridge at such fares as might be likely to tempt persons who, having no regard for Sundays themselves, would inflict their presence on the University on that day of rest ... The contemplated arrangements were as distasteful to the University authorities as they must be to Almighty God and to all right minded Christians'.

The law regarding Sunday trains was not repealed until 1908, although before then it had ceased to be observed. When the Prince of Wales was in residence, Queen Victoria approved the restrictions placed upon students. There were seven down trains and six up trains on weekdays. One 'quick train' each day did the journey in 1 hour 50 minutes. In the early trains, some passengers sat on benches in unroofed carriages. Other carriages had a roof but uncushioned seats and large unglazed side openings. Later, third-class carriages for 50 persons had only two small windows.

It was many years before there was a reliable service. Some trains started and then returned, others arrived hours late. These vicissitudes were noted by *Punch:* 'On Wednesday last a respectably dressed young man was seen to go to the Shoreditch terminus of the Eastern Counties Railway and deliberately take a ticket for Cambridge. He has not been heard of since. No motive has been assigned for the rash act.'

A local newspaper said that 'The curiosity of our fellow townsmen in the humble walks of life seems as if it never would be sated. Night after night crowds of both sexes congregate in the vicinity of the railway station to watch the arrival and departure of the evening trains. About half past seven it is even betting between the up train and the down train which shall get first into the station, so that the vacant ground on either side has its occupants, looking along the line for a curl of steam to herald the arrival.'

There was much criticism because only one platform had been provided: 'We receive complaints innumerable concerning the inconveniencies and bad management at the Railway Station in this town ... Perhaps the greatest grievance at present is that which arises from having only a single line of rails within the station itself. Before experience proved the excessive inconvenience to passengers of this arrangement, ordinary intelligence set it down as an absurdity; and the managers of the line, as if for the very purpose of making the absurdity the more palpable, have so ingeniously arranged the time bill that the rule is for an up train and a down train to arrive here nearly at the same time.'

The Great Northern Railway was anxious to reach Cambridge and promoted several Bills which envisaged stations near the Botanic Garden or on Coe Fen. The latter was opposed by the university because the line would pass 'under the windows of St Peter's College and at the back of the University'. It is fortunate that this scheme was defeated, because a line along the Backs of the Colleges would have ruined this most attractive part of Cambridge.

When the Great Northern line reached Shepreth, the company ran four-horse omnibuses from an office in Trinity Street to connect with their trains. In 1864 they promoted a Bill for either a new line to Cambridge or for running powers over the G.E.R., with a line from the station to a new G.N. station in the area bounded by Orchard Street and Emmanuel Road. The Borough Council supported this scheme, but it was opposed by the Master of Christ's who said that a goods and coal depot there would 'render Christ's and Emmanuel Colleges almost uninhabitable by the continual howling and whistling of engines'.

While this Bill was being debated, the two companies came to terms, and the G.N. secured running powers between Shepreth and Cambridge, with a separate platform and booking-office at the existing station. After a long battle, the G.N. reached Cambridge in 1866.

A newspaper of 1 November 1845, said 'Goodbye to the Stage Coach. We have seen the last of those elegant conveyances, the London coaches, upon which Cambridge used to look with pride. Last Saturday the Beehive ran its last stage; the contest against all-potent steam was found to be useless, and the reins were given up after a struggle of a few months. We are glad to record that the victor has been at least merciful, for Wilkins, the civil driver of the Beehive, has been provided for by a berth upon the rail.'

*   *   *

Prince Albert was installed as Chancellor in 1847, and on 5 July he arrived with the Queen by special train. Civic officials met the royal couple in the richly decorated station and joined a procession of the Whittlesey Yeomanry and the band of the Royal Corps of Sappers and Miners which went by Hills Road, Lensfield Road, and Trumpington Street, where an enormous triumphal arch had been erected, to Trinity College.

In the Hall, the Queen sat on a throne while the Prince read an address, and Honorary Degrees were conferred in the Senate House. They dined with Dr Philpott, the Vice-Chancellor, at Catharine Hall, the gates having been removed so that they could drive into the court. Later in the evening there was a concert in the Senate House, and a display of fireworks on Parker's Piece.

On the following day, in the Senate House, the Queen and the Prince heard prize poems and the Installation Ode written by Wordsworth, and in the afternoon attended a Grand Horticultural Show in the grounds of Downing, then visited the Fitzwilliam Museum. At 6 p.m. Mr Green, jnr., ascended from Parker's Piece in a balloon, and in the evening there was a grand banquet in Trinity. On the third day, over 4,000 people attended a public breakfast in Nevile's Court, and danced in a large marquee erected in the grounds of St John's.

*   *   *

Finch's Walk, the footpath from the end of Brooklands Avenue along Hobson's Stream, was so-named because Charles Finch, Mayor in 1849, was treasurer of a fund raised in 1861 to erect a monument at Nine Wells, where springs forming the Little New River issue from the Gog Magog Hills. For more than 100 years the Finch family was among the leading commercial firms in the town. The first member came from Dudley, Worcestershire in 1688 to take over an iron business in Market Hill, and throughout the eighteenth century the firm obtained supplies of iron from relatives in Dudley and Birmingham.

Their foundry, situated where the Lodge and Chapel of St John's now stand, and moved later to Thompson's Lane, manufactured the heavy castings which, before the days of railways, had to be made locally. These included Magdalene Bridge, the former Silver Street Bridge, and the small bridges over the Little New River at Brookside.

In 1849, the General Board of Health reported that although two and a half miles of sewers had been constructed during the previous 25 years, this had been done to no general plan and without the assistance of an engineer, so that 'from some circumstances unexplained they have not yet been rendered generally available for the reception of house sewage'. The Board also said that there were over 1,000 houses in 140 alleys, passages, or yards, some only two and a half feet wide.

NINE

The Later Nineteenth Century, 1850-1870

A spectacular fire in 1849 in the rectangular block of houses on the Market Hill destroyed eight of them, the fire-fighters being able to obtain water only from the Conduit and the river at Garret Hostel Bridge. In the following year, the Corporation obtained an Act to acquire the whole block, the remaining houses were demolished, portions of Great St Mary's churchyard were taken, and the Market was converted to its present form in 1855.

It was thought that a more impressive fountain should be erected in the centre, and this was put up at the sole charge of the Corporation, except that the tanks and flushing apparatus beneath were paid for by the Improvement Commissioners. Hobson's Conduit was removed to the corner of Lensfield Road.

H. A. Morgan, a freshman at Jesus in 1849, could see from his rooms the corpse of a man hanged on Castle Hill. Carriers carts brought hundreds of people into Cambridge for the spectacle, and Midsummer Common was crowded. Throughout Queen Victoria's reign there were annual visits of menageries. The best-known showman was Wombwell, and the animals were exhibited on St Andrew's Hill until the first Corn Exchange was built there in 1842: the menageries then moved to Midsummer Common.

In 1851 the market for hay and straw, cattle and livestock, was removed from the vicinity of St Clement's church to Honey Hill, and the post office moved to new premises at 4 St Andrew's Street on the site of the Brazen George Inn. The turnpike gate at the borough boundary on Huntingdon Road was removed in 1852.

One of the efforts originated by members of the university to assist working-class youths was the establishment in 1855 of a Working Men's College in rooms above a gymnasium. The Rev. Harvey Goodwin, then vicar of St Edward's, was appointed Principal, and in the first year there were 186 pupils who could study English, history, mathematics, Latin, French, or drawing. Charles Kingsley described the college in the preface to *Alton Locke:* 'There we have a school of a hundred men or more, taught for the last eight years gratuitously by men of the highest attainments in the University – by a dean, by professors, tutors, prizemen, men who are now headmasters of public schools, who have given freely to their fellow men knowledge which has cost them large sums of money and the labour of many years.' Interest in the College waned after a time and it ceased to function in 1865.

In 1850, less than half of the undergraduates read for honours, and the course for the ordinary degree was of a very low standard. Mathematical studies were still paramount, and in 1851, 116 students gained honours in mathematics, only 38 in classics. Many gifted men like Lord Macaulay, who was in residence from 1818-24, could only gain an ordinary degree because they could not pass the mathematical examination.

Among the Masters, Whewell of Trinity, 1841-66, was a leading figure who advocated moderate reforms. He was said to be astonishingly knowledgeable, and seemed able to talk with authority on any subject, but immured himself in his Lodge and did not associate with either Fellows or students. The Trinity Fellows complained that he was 'arbitrary, unconciliatory, and sometimes excessively rude'. A Board of Mathematical Studies was established, and two new triposes, one in the natural sciences, and the other in moral sciences, including history, jurisprudence, and English law, were instituted in 1848.

By 1852, the town electorate consisted of 1,850 householders and 37 freemen. Both of the political parties practised bribery and corruption, and an election cost a candidate about £1,000. Many of the bribed electors were so uneducated that they could not even write their name. A new Guildhall was begun in 1859, when the large Assembly Room was built, and in 1895 a wing in Guildhall Street was added.

*   *   *

By the middle of the nineteenth century, when there were about 1,600 undergraduates, many of them resented the restrictions imposed by the colleges, and the more serious students found much of the teaching inadequate. The Graham Commission of 1852 reported that students 'are at an age when they cannot be submitted to the minute surveillance and rigid constraint exercised in a school', they had to be subjected to 'so much constraint as may guard the inexperienced against the temptations of youth and the dangers of wasteful extravagance; so much liberty, as may serve to develop the qualities of their moral character, and prepare them gradually for the weightier responsibilities and fuller freedom of after life'.

In the nineteenth century, about one-third of the undergraduates were the sons of clergymen, and several of the colleges gave preference to them or to boys who intended to go into the church. At Corpus, between 1822 and 1880, most of the students took holy orders. Attendance at chapel was compulsory, and most deans insisted that the men were present at least four or five times a week, providing that they went to both the morning and the evening service on Sundays.

At least one don opposed these practices. In 1834 Connop Thirlwall, an assistant tutor at Trinity, issued a pamphlet in which he attacked compulsory chapel, 'the constant repetition of a heartless, mechanical service,' and said that 'with an immense majority of our congregation it is not a religious service at all, and that to the remaining few it is the least impressive and edifying that can be conceived'. For publishing this pamphlet, Connop Thirlwall was forced to resign.

At St John's, in 1852, morning chapel was at 7 on weekdays, evening chapel at 6, and in the October term the freshmen, for whom there was not sufficient space, had to attend at 5.15. Undergraduates had to be present seven times a week, though two Sunday attendances were counted as three.

Earlier, in 1838, the Trinity College authorities required eight attendances a week, and offenders could be sent down for one or more terms or even permanently. Some of the students formed a 'Society for the Prevention of Cruelty to Undergraduates,' kept a record of the attendance of the Fellows, and published it in a weekly paper circulating in Cambridge and London. In one issue they wrote: 'The Society regret much that during the past week great laxity has prevailed among the

Fellows in general with regard to their attendance in Chapel. This is the more to be lamented, as they had been for the two previous weeks so much more regular than usual. This irregularity cannot proceed from ill health, for they have been constantly to Hall, although they are not compelled to go there more than five times each week.'

Tables of the average attendances of Fellows were published at the end of a month. One had a zero after his name. In a footnote the Society asked 'Why then do they not set us a better example?' Six weeks after the introduction of the new regulation, the Master and seniors climbed down somewhat by announcing that six chapels a week would suffice, and the Society discontinued their 'Chapel Lists'. As a final shot, they published a Class List dividing the Fellows into four classes. Only three were placed in Class 1, and at the foot of the table two names were printed in italics, indicating that they were unworthy of being classed at all.

Dr Perry, who became Bishop of Melbourne, was given a prize medal and a handsome Bible, although the Society wrote that 'It is, therefore, to be hoped Mr. Perry will be more regular and do still better next term. With respect to the two Gentlemen who are not classed, the Secretary need hardly say that he does not envy them their feelings on the present occasion.' Dr Perry was one of the dons who did social work in the Barnwell district, and he paid for the rebuilding of Great St Andrew's church and for the construction of two new churches, Christ Church in Newmarket Road, and St Paul's in Hills Road.

The college and university regulations had been devised when boys were much younger. Most freshmen were now 18 or 19 and objected to being treated as schoolboys. Those who rebelled against compulsory chapel, and other restrictions, could be punished by gating, rustication, or expulsion.

Few sermons were preached in the college chapels, and afternoon services at Great St Mary's attracted crowded congregations. Many undergraduates, after their college evening services on Sundays, went to parish churches to listen to sermons. Harvey Goodwin, vicar of St Edward's was very popular because he was so sincere and spoke in a terse and pithy manner. He coached in mathematics, and was cheered by undergraduates whenever he appeared in the Senate House.

At Trinity, lectures for Freshmen were from 9 until 11 and at St John's, men had to attend two lectures daily at first, later, three in two days. There were no college lecture-rooms, and Tutors had to put desks and benches in their own rooms during term.

A man who came up to St John's in 1852 wrote that 'The college seemed to be under the impression that all Freshmen had come from rather second-rate schools,' and he found that the scripture lessons, for example, were more suitable for a Sunday School class. At Caius, a mathematician lectured on theology. On one occasion he dealt with the miracle of the healing of the paralytic recorded by St Mark, explaining that 'As the subject was called a young man he could not have been quite grown up. On the other hand, as it took four men to carry him, he could not have been very young; whence we may conclude that he was something between the two.'

The instruction given in sixth forms had improved, but colleges had not taken account of this change and the undergraduates often found lectures boring, to a large extent a repetition of what they already knew. Some colleges had only one Tutor; in Trinity there were three. Tutors usually decided who should be admitted, and arranged the teaching programme. They were supposed to concern themselves with the physical and moral welfare of students, and some did so admirably, but most undergraduates found the tutorial arrangements unsatisfactory.

From the late 1850's, some Tutors began to take an interest in the leisure activities of their men and encouraged sports, especially rowing. Leslie Stephen of Trinity Hall wrote the college boating song and took the chair at bump suppers. The majority of the dons, however, showed no interest in either their academic or personal problems. Few of the young Fellows could hope to become a Tutor or college lecturer, so the majority did not remain long, though some of the less ambitious took holy orders and waited for a college living to become vacant.

At St John's, in 1852, there were about 270 undergraduates and about 50 'Ten-Year Men,' men in holy orders who had had their name on the college books for 10 years, and who by residing for three terms could, until 1858, proceed, by keeping an Act, to the B.D. Degree. There were 53 ordinary Fellows, 8 Bye-Fellows, and all except two who were studying law and two studying medicine had to take holy orders within six years of becoming M.A.s; and in due course take a B.D. Degree. Twenty-one of the Fellowships were restricted to men from particular counties, dioceses, places, or schools.

The majority of the undergraduates did not take the Honours Examination which was restricted to two subjects and necessitated intense study, but took only the Ordinary Degree. These 'poll' or 'pass' men included those noble or wealthy men who had no academic ambitions. A man of moderate means who had to secure a Fellowship as a first step towards a career in politics, a learned profession, or the public schools, had to do well in a Tripos. As the colleges did not provide adequate teaching, he was obliged to go to a private coach. Official university and college teaching posts were limited in number, and most resident Fellows became coaches for at least a time, some to secure more income, others because it helped to pass the time. Some of the coaches were men debarred from a Fellowship because they had married.

Those who were most successful in preparing men to gain high academic honours were able to command the highest fees. Some coached a dozen men for several hours a week, and the best could earn £700-£800 a year, or what was then an average middle-class income. William Hopkins is said to have claimed that he had coached 200 men who had become Wranglers, and Edward John Routh coached over 600 students from 1855-88.

Until 1851, King's undergraduates could obtain degrees without an examination. The college had large endowments, but maintained only a few scholars, sometimes numbering less than 20. Until 1865 the Provost acted as Tutor, then the Rev. Augustus Austen Leigh was appointed Tutor in 1867. He was one of the more enlightened dons who opened their rooms to undergraduates and took an interest in their sporting activities.

The college was composed almost exclusively of former Eton boys who were foundation scholars and, later, Fellows. Relations between seniors and students were closer than in other colleges, and some Fellows returned to Eton as masters. E. F. Benson has thus described the privileged position of King's men: 'Indeed from the age of twelve or thereabouts they lived on the bounty of the pious Founder, King Henry VI, in quiet scholastic competence, most of them without duties, to the end of their days. They had their rooms provided for them, their Commons and their dinner, and a salary of several hundred pounds a year, because they got a Scholarship at Eton in their teens. The system gave them the leisure of the lilies of the field, freed them from any care concerning the necessities and moderate luxuries of life, and while they could thus devote their whole time to scholarly research they could equally well do nothing at all ... Young men came up yearly from Eton, and in time grew into old men among them. One of these, for instance, lived since his earliest manhood in a set of Fellow's rooms from which he never emerged except in the evening gloaming. He then shuffled out on to the big lawn with a stick in his hand, and prodded the worms with it, muttering to himself, 'Ah, damn ye; ye haven't got me yet,' and then returned to his rooms until the same hour next day.'

Bishop Abraham, writing in 1851, said that 'No man can doubt that it was a bad thing for us being excluded from the university society and honours. It narrowed and dwarfed our moral and intellectual growth; we became exclusive and bumptious about nothing but our supposed privileges, which were really evils.' Oscar Browning wrote: 'Our Society was peculiar in many ways; we consorted with no other college except Jesus, then a small college like ourselves, and our friendship was celebrated by an annual cricket match. We were great at breakfast-parties, given at 9 a.m., after chapel and Shilleto's lecture. The bill of fare – fish, solid meat and game, beer the only liquid consumed. They lasted two hours or more. A favourite amusement of ours was riding, and we often scampered over the fields, a merry cavalcade. But walks with chosen friends were our main resource.'

*   *   *

Soon after the installation of the Prince Consort as Chancellor in 1847, he advocated that the scope of studies should be widened, and some graduates and former members of the university asked the Prime Minister to appoint a Royal Commission. A Report of 1852 stated that the annual income of the colleges was £185,000, and that of the university only £18,000, and that colleges ought to make contributions to the university to provide lecture-rooms, laboratories, and additional professors and lecturers. Because the smaller colleges could not provide efficient teaching, men had to rely upon private coaches, therefore the standard of lecturing must be improved. All main subjects should have a Board of Studies, and honours courses in modern languages and civil engineering should be provided.

The Cambridge University Act of 1856 appointed eight commissioners to revise university and college statutes, established a Council of the Senate and new Boards of Studies. Religious tests were abolished for men taking degrees in the arts, law, medicine, and music. Professors were required to reside in Cambridge, and laymen could hold college posts. These reforms enhanced the reputation of the university, and the average number of freshmen rose from about 400 in 1850 to almost twice as many by 1880.

An attempt to settle the disputes between the university and the town was made in 1855 when Lord Palmerston, who was then Home Secretary, suggested that Sir John Patteson should arbitrate between the parties. His award became an Act of Parliament in 1856. The Town Council had given evidence about various privileges of the university that they wanted to have abolished, and the Act deprived the university of the power to license alehouses, and to supervise weights and measures, markets and fairs.

The Vice-Chancellor retained his right to license theatres, and occasional entertainments had to be approved both by him and the Mayor. The Black Assembly and the Mayor's oath to maintain the privileges of the university were abolished. University property and college chapels and libraries were exempted from parochial rates, but other college property was rated. A Watch Committee of nine town and five university members would control the police, and the contribution of the university under the Improvement Acts was reduced from two-thirds to one-quarter. The Proctors retained powers to arrest women suspected of being prostitutes, who were tried by the Vice-Chancellor sitting in the Spinning House, and those convicted were imprisoned there.

In January 1860, some undergraduates invited Cambridge girls to an evening party at the De Freville Arms, Great Shelford, and hired an omnibus to transport the guests and a small band. Edmund Blore, a Pro-Proctor, learned about this, and also that the innkeeper had been asked to provide breakfast on the following morning. Convinced therefore that the girls were being invited for an improper purpose, he and the Senior Proctor and their 'bulldogs' stopped the omnibus as it passed Parker's Piece, and ordered it to proceed to the Spinning House. There the Vice-Chancellor sentenced five of the women to be imprisoned. Emma Kemp received the most severe sentence of 14 days because she

Opposite top: *Cambridge Gambols at Peter House, by T. Rowlandson, from* **Gradus ad Cantabrigiam,** *1844*

Opposite bottom: *The Battle of Peas Hill, 1820, from* **Gradus ad Cantabrigiam,** *1844*

had been accompanied by her younger sister who was only 14. She was released after five days, and later brought an unsuccessful action against the Vice-Chancellor.

At this period, clergymen wore white starched neck-cloths, while laymen tied coloured scarves round their neck. Some wore a blue coat with brass buttons. The wealthier men had cut-away coats, stocks, embroidered waistcoats and peg-top trousers. Moustaches were not allowed, but most had mutton cutlet-type whiskers. Beards and moustaches were later worn by members of the Volunteer Movement. Caps and gowns were worn in the streets, and older dons were shocked when a few Fellows began to appear in an old flannel suit.

Darwin's *Origin of Species* (1860) called into question many fundamental Christian dogmas, and many dons were troubled. In the later 'sixties, Henry Sidgwick was outstanding, an advocate of the abolition of religious tests and for the provision of scholarships and fellowships for natural science. He vigorously supported better educational facilities for women.

Dinner in Trinity is described by Sir Richard Claverhouse Jebb: 'Have you ever seen our hall at Trinity during feeding time? Fancy a vast hall, traversed lengthwise by narrow tables. Fancy these tables crowded to excess with British youths in every stage of starvation or repletion ... Between these tables ... fancy a dense tide of slovenly men and dirty old women pushing, wrangling, struggling for hacked and gory joints, upsetting gravy, dropping dishes, always in a hurry never attending to one, but always going to everybody. If ... you can further portray to your fancy the personal appearance of a leg of mutton, which has been carved in succession by three or four men, who have distinct and antagonistic theories on that subject, you will have a faint and dim conception of Trinity and its Hall.'

'So, last Monday, a meeting was held of some Trinity men at which a Petition was approved for presentation to Whewell and the Senior Fellows, praying earnestly for a total Reform. The Petition showed that the manner of serving dinner in hall was disgusting, and called for two dinners at different hours to prevent crowding, that a staff of men waiters cleanly, decently dressed and efficient be organised; that a man should be exempt from paying for dinner in Hall upon giving notice. The Master agreed to the Tutors suggesting reforms.'

Opposite top: *The Gate of Honour, Caius College, The Senate House and the University Library,* by G. Dodgson, *first published in the* **Cambridge University Almanack,** *1845, and reissued in 1864*
Opposite bottom: *The University Library, the Senate House and Great St Mary's Church,* by P. S. Lamborn, *1769*

Reminiscences by James Stuart also describe conditions in 1862: 'The waiting was very bad. There were certain old ladies who had the right to cater for certain tables in hall. They were obliged, I believe, to provide a certain number of lbs. of meat per head, but they had as perquisites all that was not eaten ... Inferior joints used to be passed down, and whole joints, uncut, were dropped by these old ladies into large baskets which they had with them at the end of the table.'

The dirty old women were replaced by male waiters in 1866. Charles Stuart Calverley, writing of life at Christ's in about 1860, said that 'The dinner was served at 4. It was generally very bad, consisting wholly of joints, not well roasted, with potatoes and small beer. Other things were to be had if called and paid for. Each college then brewed its own ale. After Hall the men divided into little sets and went in turn to each other's rooms and drank port or sherry till 6. At 6 Chapel. After Chapel reading men shut themselves up till 10 or so with tea and books; after 10, there were other gatherings with pipes and beer till midnight.'

The University Amateur Dramatic Club was founded in 1855 by Sir Frederick Burnand, and for five years the club rented two rooms in the Hoop Hotel. In 1860 it took over the former ballroom, lately occupied by the Union. The A.D.C. became a recognised body largely because Edward VII took a great interest while he was an undergraduate. In 1870 there were moves to suppress the club, but the efforts of J. W. Clark averted the threat. The freehold of the theatre was bought in 1882.

The building erected at St Andrew's Hill in 1842 as a Corn Exchange and then used as a covered market called The Arcade, was for a short time a music-hall, strictly out of bounds for undergraduates. There was also the small Bijou Theatre at Peas Hill. Keith and Tudor had a small circus in a wooden building on Midsummer Common, before moving to Auckland Road and, later, Romsey Town. There were several amateur minstrel troupes which claimed to provide 'fun without vulgarity'.

Cambridge still lacks an adequate concert hall and ballroom, and only in recent times acquired a large indoor swimming-pool, yet in 1857 the New Music Hall and Public Rooms Company proposed to provide these and other facilities in one building. The site of the Hoop Hotel was secured, and plans were made for a hotel with large clubroom and lecture rooms on the Bridge Street frontage. Behind this, a first-class swimming-bath entered from Jesus Lane, and a second-class bath entered from Park Street. Above the baths a concert hall to seat 2,000, with an organ, also a ballroom and restaurant. There was some opposition to this ambitious scheme, and in 1858 it was abandoned.

Five years later, in 1863, the Roman Bath Co. Ltd opened a swimming-bath, 56 feet by 22 feet in Jesus Lane, containing 28,000 gallons of water. Ladies had sole use of it from 11 until 5 on Tuesdays. The venture proved unprofitable, and the premises were let to the Pitt Club. The elaborate entrance in Jesus Lane still exists.

*   *   *

In 1859 some Cambridge men suggested that a Rifle Club should be formed to enable men to acquire skill in shooting and to encourage those who might be willing to serve their country in time of need. The proposal was welcomed by the Home Secretary, and the Cambridge Rifle Club was formed. Tennyson wrote a poem, *Riflemen, form!* printed in the *Times* and soon many other clubs were established. Two corps were formed in the town, The Cambridge University Rifle Volunteers, and The First Cambridgeshire Volunteer Rifles.

In 1861 a dense crowd attended a review on Parker's Piece, the local corps being joined by 350 men of the Inns of Court Corps. H. A. Morgan, Master of Jesus 1885-1912, joined the Volunteers and was at a parade on Parker's Piece when a new officer wrongly gave the order 'Charge with fixed bayonets.' Those in the front rank had to flee for their lives, pursued by those behind; later, he was always careful to be in the rear rank.

Tennyson was at Trinity, but did not reside in college. He had lodgings in Rose Crescent, and later opposite the Bull Hotel. Trinity was the scene of a magnificent ball when the future Edward VII came with his bride a few months after his wedding in 1864. The whole of Nevile's Court was roofed with canvas and floored to make a vast ballroom, with a band under the Library, and a banquet was provided in the Hall. The old kitchen had open ranges 6 feet high and 12 feet long, where scores of joints were roasted on huge spits.

All Saints' Church in St John's Street, with its tower which projected over the footway, was demolished in 1865. In 1860 the river was frozen for some time and the Lent boat races had to be abandoned. The university eight, unable to train on the Cam, went to Cookham, but was immobilised there for twelve days. The Free Library, which then possessed 9,398 books, was removed in 1862 to the space below the large Assembly Room of the Guildhall.

Although the railway had curtailed the river traffic, the Mill Pond was still often so crowded with barges loaded with coal, corn or oil cake, that one could step from one to the other from the mills to beyond Queens' College bridge. Granaries covered a large area between Mill Lane and Little St Mary's Lane, and waggons waiting to unload frequently completely filled these streets. The large building beside the Mill Pond was Foster's granary, later Dolby's boat-building works. Dolby married Mrs Robson of the Anchor Inn and boatyard, who bought more boats in 1895 and in 1906 leased Swan's Nest (Robinson Crusoe Island). During her lifetime, no boats were ever let out on Sundays. Mr Prime, manager of the Anchor yard, is said to have brought the first punt to Cambridge after he had seen them being used for races at Henley.

*   *   *

In the 'sixties the musical services at King's College Chapel were criticised, and the 1862 statutes ordered that choristers should be lodged, boarded and taught. In 1869 the boys were still the sons of local tradesmen, and until 1871 they had to wait at table in Hall. They received no remuneration, but free dinners, a quartern loaf of bread and a pound of cheese weekly, a suit of clothes and a cloth gown every year.

In order to attract boys of a better cultural background, temporary accommodation for boarders was secured in 1876 and a new building in West Road opened in 1878. The Provost, the Rev. Augustus Austen Leigh, took a personal interest in every boy. Choral scholarships were created, and with other volunteers Dr A. H. Mann, organist and choirmaster, established a great reputation for the musical services.

Trinity maintained a choir of ten boys and a music master, and in 1819 Trinity and St John's had agreed to share the same choir, organist, and schoolmaster. From 1856 Trinity had its own choir school in two rooms in St Michael's churchyard, and from about 1894-99 in the college, then the choristers were sent to the Perse or County schools. St John's had a small school in All Saints' Passage from 1856.

At Great St Mary's, the throne across the chancel, the western gallery and the great oak pulpit in the centre of the nave were demolished in 1863, and the nave and aisles were provided with fixed pews. A minority of the university opposed these changes, holding that the former arrangement made the preacher audible throughout the church. Dr Whewell said that the Doctors' seats in the Throne were very convenient, and that the idea that to sit back to the altar was impious, was not only fanciful but also superstitious.

* * *

Visitors who came to Cambridge in the second half of the nineteenth century to see the beauties of the colleges, were totally unaware that there were large areas of slums to the north of the town. In 1801 the village of Barnwell had 252 inhabitants. By 1821 the population had increased to 2,211, and to nearly 13,000 in 1862, the year in which the Rev. G. W. Weldon became Vicar of Christ Church. An old friend, on learning of his appointment, told him that 'It would be better for you to go among the Zulus. You have no idea of the kind of place you are going to. No undergraduate not engaged in parish work could be seen there without the taint of suspicion.'

Mr Weldon himself wrote that it would be impossible to exaggerate the low estimate in which certain areas of the parish were then held. Streets bearing such illustrious names as Wellington and Nelson were sunk in a very low state of demoralisation, every house a resort of characters of bad repute, and he had witnessed scenes, even in the open day, that could hardly be credited.

There were a few streets off East Road in which numerous prostitutes lived, where the Proctors made almost nightly visits. A refuge for girls who wished to reform was established, first at Dover Cottage in East Road, and later in a building behind Christ Church. By 1880 it had admitted 120 young women. Some Barnwell people asked the Post Office not to have letters posted in the district stamped with that name, because their friends objected to having letters from such a notorious place.

At first Mr Weldon had only one curate, but he was helped by many district visitors, and, during term, by about a hundred undergraduates. Grants from the Church Pastoral Aid Society and the University later provided enough money for seven curates, and slowly the labours of the church and social workers transformed the district. The Methodists built their first chapel, by voluntary labour, in Fitzroy Street, and the Baptists erected Zion Chapel in East Road.

In 1899 the Bishop of Ely said that Barnwell was 'a thickly thronged suburb, a dark spot close to the very focus of light. Many university servants were living there, and the evil of a large, poor and almost destitute population needed remedying.' In 1902, 400 people in St Matthew's parish were living three or more to a bedroom, and twenty houses shared a single water tap. In the parish of St Andrew the Less, 52 persons were living five or more to a bedroom, and 15 houses shared a tap.

The district which became known as Romsey Town had, in 1870, only a few dwellings and cattle grazed in the meadows. It took its name from Romsey House, a fine old mansion noted for its carved oak and pitchpine joinery and interesting chimneys, standing among trees and flowers in a garden extending from the Salisbury Club to Malta Road. When the first new houses were built beyond the railway line in 1879 the street did not have a name, and letters were addressed ' – Terrace, Mill Road, over the line.' By 1881 there were 300 inhabitants, but the district developed so rapidly that the *Cambridge Chronicle* of 7 March 1883, stated that 'The district has about 300 houses containing 1500 people. There being no surface drains, in wet weather small lakes are formed almost up to the knees. It has no sewer, the cross streets are all private ones, and most have no footpaths or carriage ways. Residents there are in a deplorable state, some having no water supply.'

At a meeting held in the Mill Road Mission Hall in 1894 it was stated that 4,000 people now lived on that side of the railway line, and in 1895 an appeal was made for help for the many families feeling very keenly the pinch of poverty and suffering the pangs of hunger in Romsey Town district. Four years later, in 1899, there were 48 streets with 1,700 houses spread over one and a half square miles, and the population had increased to 8,500. The district had two churches, three nonconformist chapels, a Railway Mission, a Salvation Army Citadel, a Friends' Meeting-House, and four schools.

In the middle of the nineteenth century there were a great many people in Cambridge who had a hard struggle to exist on an inadequate income.

As Eglantyne Jebb wrote in *Cambridge, A Brief Study in Social Questions*, 'In our streets we meet occasionally with pitiful caricatures of men and women, poor puny wastrels, starvelings, degenerates, on whose faces the dull suffering of hopelessness has left its indelible stamp, and we meet with many more to whom life has never brought its full heritage, creatures of stunted faculties, of wasted and misused gifts, of poor and mean experience, prisoners of their circumstances, ground down by the difficulties of their lot, or ruined by its dangers.'

A Cambridge man who visited the racing stables at Chantilly, near Paris, was surprised to find that half of the boys employed there came from Cambridge. A trainer explained that agents in the principal towns were employed to find boys of 14 who were backward in physical development and who had a taste for betting and racing, and that more such boys were found in Cambridge than in any other town in England.

Many persons of the prosperous and leisured classes, some of them members of the university, recognised the serious social problems, and there was a marked increase in philanthropic activity. Numerous societies were established to tackle different aspects of the problems. Among the societies founded to assist working-class boys were the Y.M.C.A., The Boys' Brigade, The Church Lads' Brigade, Naval Crusaders, The Cambridge Boys' Mission, and a number of parochial clubs. For girls there was the Y.W.C.A., The Girls' Friendly Society, The Free Church Girls' Guild, and the Cambridge Association for the Care of Girls.

The Charity Organisation Society was formed to co-ordinate the efforts of these various societies and private individuals, and its members visited the homes of people in distress to ascertain the circumstances and the best means of giving assistance. Almshouses and endowments were subject to parochial restrictions, and most could only help the poor of the parishes in the older part of the town, although these contained less than a quarter of the population. Until 1856, when there was a common Poor Law fund, each parish was responsible for its own poor. In 1900 the civil parishes were amalgamated and called the parish of Cambridge.

The Rev. A. E. Humphrey, Superintendent of the Jesus Lane Sunday School, decided to use a classroom on two evenings a week for the instruction and amusement of members of the Bible class, and this was the origin of the Cambridge Youths' Club for boys between 14 and 20. In 1867, a large two-storeyed building with two reading-rooms, three

classrooms and a gymnasium, was erected in Paradise Street. Charles
Kingsley, one of the early helpers, wrote that it was 'an admirable thing
got up by High Church bachelors and undergraduates for getting hold of
shopmen and middle-class lads'.

Instruction was given in reading, writing, arithmetic, book-keeping,
shorthand, French, and Latin. A drum and fife band later became a brass
band, and there was a minstrel party. The sporting activities of the club
were outstanding, and Sir Jack Hobbs was perhaps the most famous
member. There were successful cricket, football, gymnastics, athletics, and
harriers teams, and the club put two eights on the river. In 1876 the name
was changed to The Albert Institute, and new buildings were opened a
year later.

The first floor of the Paradise Street building was occupied in 1871 by
the Higher Grade Boys' School and opened with 15 boys. A girls'
school began with 20 pupils in 1873, and moved to Eden Street a year
later. The Borough Council built premises for both boys and girls in
Melbourne Place in 1913.

*   *   *

H. A. Morgan, Master of Jesus 1885-1912, aided by James Porter,
Master of Peterhouse 1876-1900, held meetings in Cambridge and
London in 1868 to support an appeal for money to improve the river,
and they raised about £450. Queen Victoria gave £100 and the Prince
of Wales £50. The Masters said that owing to the cessation of barge
traffic combined with increased sewerage, 3 to 4 feet of mud had formed
at the bottom of the river, and there was only 2 feet of water in some
places, making it unfit for rowing. By 1870 the river had been deepened
and widened, and the Great Eastern Railway agreed to erect a new
bridge costing about £1,750. These measures had a good effect on
Cambridge rowing, as Cambridge crews won the boat race for five
consecutive years.

The university abolished religious tests in 1871, except for Masters
and candidates for divinity degrees, but the Roman Catholic authorities
did not allow students to come to Cambridge until 1895. Lyttelton,
writing of conditions in 1874, said that 'Although each freshman was
assigned to a tutor, our relations were purely formal, and I have no

recollection of a single word of advice from any don in the place. The moral tone of the college was such as to be expected. Some of us were grievously perplexed at hearing that three responsible dons were often the worse for liquor.'

'Disgusting orgies by a set of young fools kept the Beef Steak Club going, the club's only purpose being the provision of drunken parties at stated intervals. There was a large ingredient of the 'Jesus Lane lot' who lodged in that locality and spent the whole of their time roystering, not one of them ever attempting to read for a degree. Thus the undergraduates were exposed to temptations, to self-indulgence, largely condoned by most dons, sloth, degrading conversation, drinking clubs and idleness on the part of a number of Public School men ... A few voices were raised against idleness, but in 1874 it is undeniable that the building up of strong, clean and high-minded characters was made difficult by the blindness of dons to evils into which many youngsters fell against their will.'

The small iron bridge between the grounds of Trinity and St John's was built in 1874. On Sundays, many Fellows rode out to take services in villages, and returned late. At some colleges where suppers were not provided, they formed Sunday evening clubs. Known as The Curates' Club at St John's, The Neck or Nothing at King's, they supped off mutton chops. Supper at the Christ's club, The Apostolic, was always tripe.

Townsmen, and not undergraduates, were responsible for the Shah of Persia Hoax in 1873. The Mayor received a telegram purporting to come from Crewe, where the Shah was staying, stating that His Excellency intended to visit Cambridge. The Mayor promptly informed the members of the Corporation and the Vice-Chancellor, and hasty arrangements were made for a luncheon, the Volunteers were summoned by bugle, and the Mayor and Corporation in their robes of office, preceded by mace-bearers, and representatives of the university, went to the station. The platform was crowded with important people, and the Town Clerk was ready with an address of welcome. The train arrived, but no Shah alighted, and the dignitaries realised that they had been hoaxed. Robes were hastily discarded and taken back to the Guildhall in a brake, but the Volunteers, with their band playing, marched back through the streets. In the evening it was learned that the Shah had actually been attending a royal garden party.

At the beginning of the Michaelmas term in 1878, posters announced that the Theatre Royal at Barnwell would re-open under new management. People who went there expecting to see a play found a prayer meeting; the Hon. Keith Falconer had bought the building to make it into a mission hall. When it became the Festival Theatre in 1926, a lantern outside the stage door still had GOD IS LOVE on one side, and ALL HAVE SINNED on the other.

*   *   *

There must be many Cambridge people who can recall the popular Concerts which took place on Saturday evenings, when for a penny one could hear local vocalists, organ recitals, or watch conjurers, etc. These began in 1880 when at a meeting in the rooms of the Rev. F. Wallis, Dean of Caius, it was decided to book the Guildhall for most Saturdays in the term, and a committee was appointed to secure the co-operation of college musical societies and others willing to help.

On 7 March 1874, the *Cambridge Chronicle* announced that 'The long-felt want of a public conveyance between Cambridge and these villages (Grantchester and Trumpington) is at last supplied. A vehicle starts at 2 p.m. from Senate House Hill. Mr. Moore, proprietor.' In the following year a new Corn Exchange was erected.

*   *   *

H. A. Morgan played an important part in a serious riot of 1875.

The disorderly conduct of many students was a source of great annoyance to the townspeople, and the Mayor, John Death, had as chief magistrate attempted to check the rowdiness and had aroused the hostility of the undergraduates. Matters came to a head when students broke up a concert held in the Corn Exchange in the presence of the Mayor and Corporation. Seven students were arrested, and on the next evening students paraded the streets and burnt an effigy of the Mayor on the Market Hill.

On the morning of the third day, when it became known that heavy fines had been inflicted on the seven accused men, a crowd rushed to

Poplar House, the Mayor's residence, then on the present site of the Wesleyan Chapel at 'Four Lamps'. All of the windows were broken, and much damage done in the neighbourhood. A constable went to fetch H. A. Morgan, then Tutor of Jesus, who was known to be popular with the undergraduates. He was cheered when he appeared and, standing on a wall, began: 'You young scoundrels, you ought to be ashamed of yourselves frightening a lot of women out of their wits.' He concluded that he would be quite blind for five minutes, but no longer, during which they should disperse. Such was the power of his personality, that the mob gave three cheers for him and went away. The police and the proctors took no further action, and in commemoration of his deliverance, the Mayor presented him with a large piece of silver plate.

* * *

In the older college buildings, staircases led to rooms to the left and right on each floor. The rooms had no separate toilet or sanitary arrangements, and an army of bedmakers was needed to tidy the rooms, carry up coal for fires and water for jugs and basins, assisted by menservants called gyps. J. W. Clark wrote 'When I came up to Trinity in 1852, baths were unknown in college rooms. We used foot-tubs, and basins and so forth. In the following year some enterprising youngster, in advance of his time, brought a bath into college, and insisted on his bedmaker filling it every morning from the fountain in Great Court. Great was the indignation felt, and expressed, by those venerable ladies, and there might perhaps have been a general strike if a timely concession had not been made by laying on the Water Company's supply to the different staircases.'

In 1871, St Catharine's purchased 70 Trumpington Street and constructed a swimming-bath in an old cellar. Caius built baths in the basement of St Michael's Court in 1904, added more in 1907 in Tree Court, and in 1909 in the basement of the north-west corner of Gonville Court. B. L. Manning, who entered Jesus in 1912, has recorded that there were then no bathrooms, and one used a kind of big tin saucer in the bedrooms, filled by the bedmakers with cold water from the kitchen. Baths were not built until 1922.

Many of the bedmakers were widows with a family to support, or respectable elderly spinsters. They were regarded as socially superior to the townswomen who worked as ordinary charladies. Some were employed throughout the year, others only during terms. Social workers of the period sometimes found that the husband of a bedmaker gave working himself when his wife secured a permanent college post. The earnings of the woman gave the man less incentive to work, and it was said that the Oxford system, where men were employed on work similar to that undertaken by the bedmakers in Cambridge, had a better result upon the homes of college servants.

Everett, writing in 1866, describes the immense powers of the bedmakers. 'Nominally, there is one assigned to every eight rooms, and she has one assistant under her. Practically, a person once appointed to this seriously lucrative and responsible place never gives it up, although utterly superannuated, toothless, and tottering . . . Now, these good ladies are much more in possession of your premises than you are yourself. They have a key to get into your room at all hours . . . They constitute themselves inspectresses-general over all your belongings and arrangements . . . You are hopelessly in their power, and have your choice of submitting quietly to their ultra-despotic rule, or of carrying on a constant warfare.' Everett mentions the food which they obtained as perquisites, and 'You not only are charged a handsome sum in your bill for their care of rooms, but another separate charge for their beer money.'

These women were often rough and crude, but many looked after their gentlemen with maternal solicitude. One of them, on disturbing a man in his tin bath, cried 'Lor, sir, don't mind me. I'm a mother myself.' A student who found his bedmaker reading one of his letters to her assistant said that she screamed and fled, but came back later to apologise. Told that it did not matter as it was not a very important letter, she said 'No sir, but it's the principle as I objects to.'

The lodgings licensed by the university were mainly in certain central streets like Jesus Lane, Malcolm Street, Portugal Place, or Green Street. Most of them were two-three storey terrace houses with a basement kitchen in which the host family lived. The university authorities insisted that doors and ground floor windows had to be secured by 10 p.m. and men staying out later had to be reported to the college. College gates were closed at 10 p.m., but admittance could be gained until midnight by ringing a bell to summon the porter. After that, latecomers had to scale the high college walls crested with broken glass or murderous spikes.

There were many rich young men who could indulge every sort of luxury. They dressed extravagantly, had costly dinners, kept horses in the college stables, frequented the races at Newmarket, and some were said to spend as much as £1,000 a year. All of the shops gave long credit, and the tradesmen had to charge high prices to make up for the bad debts of many young noblemen and gentlemen. It was said that this raised the level of prices for everyone.

Everett says that the Fellow-Commoners 'have the privilege of sitting in hall and chapel with the fellows on condition of wearing this very conspicuous gown, of paying nominally twice, and really three times as much for all college expenses ... Noblemen, or the eldest sons of noblemen, have literally to pay four times as much for all regular college expenses, and are fleeced in a hundred other ways.'

The porters, gyps and bootblacks had to be regularly supplied with beer money. When a man had passed an examination, college servants called to offer their congratulations and of course expected a tip. College porters went to the post office to collect all incoming mail for their college, and then charged $\frac{1}{2}$d a letter (half as much as the normal postage) to deliver it to a man's rooms. It was not possible to collect one's mail from the porter's lodge.

The richer undergraduates, on coming to Cambridge, brought their own silver, cutlery, linen, and wine. Those who had rooms out of college could have their lunches brought to them from the college kitchen by men who carried on their head a large tray covered with green baize. College servants often made four separate journeys to each address with the courses of the meal. A man who ordered chicken would get the whole bird. Later, a man arrived with a large wicker basket on wheels to collect the soiled crockery.

The servants in the larger lodging-houses who cooked and cleaned, lit fires, carried coals, ran baths, cleaned shoes and brushed clothes, earned 7s. 6d. a week plus their keep, the wages not being paid until the end of term.

There were many wine parties between hall and evening chapel. Small bands of musicians toured the central streets, and when they found a wine party in progress they would ring the bell and offer their services. Some Tutors and Fellows gave wine parties for undergraduates. A few of the dons could make a young man feel at ease, but others behaved in such a formal manner that their guests remained shy and embarrassed.

A. C. Benson, later Master of Magdalene, records that 'Entertaining the fair sex was, of course, strictly forbidden; nevertheless, occasionally a charmer was smuggled into rooms and even into the college itself, though liable to be arrested and cast into the Spinning House.' Benson's book, *From a College Window,* had a large sale in America, and a porter remarked that many Americans called at the college. 'To enquire about the Pepysian Library, I suppose?' he was asked. 'Lor, no sir, they all of 'em ask to see the college window.'

Many Cambridge women earned a living by doing washing for the colleges. Several pieces of common land near the centre of the town were used as drying-grounds, and in 1846 a correspondent wrote to the *Cambridge Chronicle* to protest about college laundresses who dried linen across the thoroughfare between Emmanuel Lane and New Square. He alleged that it was impossible for persons to cross that portion of Christ's Pieces without damp linen and diluted soapsuds flicking in their faces.

There were three college laundries in Granta Place and Little St Mary's Lane. At 1 Granta Place, a widow with two sons and two daughters, helped by several hired women, did all the washing for two colleges in the small four-roomed house. The eldest son fetched the linen in a handcart, and the washing was done in the kitchen and a small penthouse. Coe Fen was the drying ground, people erecting their own posts, but paying a fee of a shilling a year to the Corporation.

The two daughters did the ironing in the bedrooms, and mangling was performed on a large machine like a double bed, weighted with large stones, in a penthouse across the road at the rear of the King's Mill. When Peterhouse introduced electric lighting, the women using Coe Fen protested that smoke emitted during the making of the electricity deposited soot on their clean linen. Some college laundry went by carriers' carts to the villages.

*   *   *

In some colleges, a Fellow could retain his fellowship after marriage; in others, this was only allowed if he also held an office in the university as a professor, librarian, etc. Colleges had been endowed by founders and benefactors with the right to appoint men to church livings all over the country, and some Fellows became engaged in the hope that a college living might soon become vacant. Sometimes the girls were kept waiting for a very long time because some aged clergyman was such a long time dying.

One Fellow who went to a country parish did not tell his college that he had married, so that the emoluments of the fellowship continued to be paid to him. The first that the college knew about it was when his widow wrote to express the hope that they would continue to her the little annuity that they had so kindly paid to her recently deceased husband.

*　　*　　*

Undergraduates began to play golf on Coe Fen in 1872, and three years later moved to a nine-hole course on Coldham's Common, a rough and muddy area where the hazards included deep ditches and grazing cattle. The town rifle range extended down the centre of the course, and golf balls sometimes had to be retrieved under rifle or machine-gun fire. The club was not allowed to play during the third term because the grass was cut for hay. In 1887 the course was altered to 18 holes and a clubhouse was built, and in 1901 the C.U. Golf Club made arrangements to play at Mildenhall.

An advertisement in the *Cambridge Chronicle* of 25 January 1895 announced 'GOLF! GOLF! GOLF! Gray's Golf Links will be formally opened for play (9 holes) on Thursday next, January 31, 1895. The course is situated in the Grantchester Meadows.' The *Cambridge Review* said: 'It is intended to memorialise the District Council against the New Golf Course in Grantchester Meadows, as interfering with the freedom of way, and exposing passengers of all classes to much danger from the balls. It has been signed by many Grantchester inhabitants. We confess we feel considerable sympathy with the protest, as the new course will seriously interfere with the pleasantest of the walks round Cambridge.'

*　　*　　*

Monstrous vehicles with four wheels called velocipedes appeared in 1859, and one writer of the time said that by hard work they could travel at about six miles an hour. Lord Dunedin claimed that he was the first undergraduate to ride a bicycle, and the first M.P. to ride one into Palace Yard. The Hon. Keith Falconer, who entered Trinity in 1874, became famous when he won a ten-mile race in 34 minutes, beating all previous records. He won several other races as well. In a five-mile race at Cambridge in 1878 he defeated the professional champion, and a contemporary record says that 'The excitement was something indescribable. Such a neck and neck race was never heard of. The pace for the last mile was terrific. He had beaten the fastest rider in the world.'

There were Oxford and Cambridge cycling races, and the university had a 'bicycle ground' in Madingley Road. The firm of Howes had been founded early in the century as coachbuilders and wheelwrights. In the 1850's the son of the founder visited the Paris Exhibition and brought back a 'boneshaker'. Cycles became the main interest of the firm, and they manufactured 'Granta' cycles. M. R. James, Provost of King's, says: 'At the end of 1884 Hugh Childers and I hired a strange machine called a Cheylesmore double tricycle, where we sat side by side, the steering gear in front, solid tyres.' In 1903 a man was fined five shillings for riding a bicycle on the footpath of Sheep's Green, the magistrate remarking that 'There is scarcely a place in Cambridge now where pedestrians can walk with safety. Cyclists are an utterly reckless class, who don't care tuppence about other people. They are the most selfish people in the world.'

In the nineties, an undergraduate, G.T. Bennett, was said to be 'the fastest thing on the road'. He won a cup for cycling 100 miles over rough roads in 10h. 54m. on a heavy machine with an experimental gear wheel. He then had a machine constructed in Cambridge to his own design. It was built to minimize wind pressure, and had two short tubes at the head of the front fork instead of handlebars. He was compelled to sit so bent that he could not see approaching traffic without strain, so a mirror was fitted to the frame.

TEN

The Later Nineteenth Century, 1870-1890

In 1858 the university instituted Local Examinations for grammar school boys, and a joint Oxford and Cambridge Board began examinations for public school boys in 1873. Lectures given in some northern towns by Cambridge dons were so successful that the university decided to extend these extra-mural activities. Cavendish College was founded in 1873 to cater for poor students, but ran into financial difficulties and had to be closed after 20 years.

Many people were demanding better educational facilities for women, and in 1867 the North of England Council for Promoting the Higher Education of Women arranged lectures at various centres and asked the universities of Oxford and Cambridge to hold examinations which would qualify girls to become teachers. Cambridge instituted a Women's Local Examination in 1868, and Henry Sidgwick headed a committee to arrange courses.

An Association for the Promotion of the Higher Education of Women in Cambridge was formed in 1873. Emily Davies set up a committee to raise money to establish a college, a house at Hitchin was rented in 1869, and some Cambridge dons travelled there to give lectures. She insisted that her students should take the normal university examinations in mathematics and classics and prove themselves as capable as the men. By 1872 the house had become too small, and some of her supporters advocated a move to Cambridge, but at first she opposed this as she was anxious to avoid any possibility of scandal.

It was decided to build the college at Girton, about two miles from the centre of the town, a site considered to be far enough away to discourage visits by male undergraduates, but near enough for dons who would lecture there in the afternoons. A small Hall and a residential block was built in 1873, and the students received most of their instruction within the college. Eventually 22 of the 34 university professors agreed to admit women to their lectures, the students being conveyed to Cambridge in carriages. For many years, chaperones were always present when male dons coached girls at Girton.

A second college for women, Newnham, began modestly in 1871 when Anne Jemima Clough supervised the first five students in a house in Regent Street, until Merton Hall was leased for resident and local students. A limited liability company was formed and Newnham Hall (now Old Hall) opened in 1875. Sidgwick Hall followed in 1880, when the Newnham College Association was inaugurated to combine the efforts of the 'Lectures Association' and the company.

St John's built a new Chapel designed by Sir George Gilbert Scott in 1864-9, a grandiose edifice unrelated to the rest of the college, and the old Chapel was then demolished. St John's Lane had been closed in 1862 by an Act of Parliament promoted jointly by the college and the Corporation. The middle of the Lane was a parish boundary, and the Chapel is in three parishes.

All undergraduates had to be a member of a college until 1869, when unattached students were admitted, controlled by a Censor. In 1893 Fitzwilliam Hall opposite the Museum became a centre for them. In 1870 Caius erected the building beside the Senate House designed by Waterhouse. It was then much admired, condemned by later generations as too assertive, but thought by some people today to be a notable example of Victorian architecture.

By 1870 the Post Office had become too small, and a larger building was constructed at the corner of Petty Cury, replacing the well-known Wrestlers' Inn, one of the most picturesque buildings in the town. There were then 11 town postmen and three college postmen, but only six pillar-boxes. In the same year the *Chronicle* reported that the wharves at Newnham were unoccupied. The railway had finally caused the abandonment of most of the river traffic, but barges still discharged firewood and peat turves at Quayside until the early part of the twentieth century.

*   *   *

Another Royal Commission reported in 1873 that of the 350 Fellows, only 120 actually lived in Cambridge and performed teaching or administrative tasks. An Act of 1877 obliged colleges to make contributions to university funds and stipulated that Fellows must hold a college or university post. Revised statutes came into force in 1882. Colleges were henceforth no longer completely independent, and the university gained in importance. More professors and lecturers were appointed, and Fellows need no longer be in holy orders nor remain celibate. They were to be elected for an initial period of six years, and Fellowships could normally only be prolonged if a man held a university or college appointment.

Some dons would not admit women to their lectures, and others ignored their presence. Sir Arthur Quiller-Couch always commenced his lectures with the word 'Gentlemen'. The Trinity College Seniority Minutes of 7 November 1879, record that 'It was proposed and carried (Ayes 5, Noes 3) that during the next Lent Term Mr. B. E. Hammond be authorized to admit to his lectures on History, if held in Lecture Room No. 15, a certain number of women, on condition that they are accompanied by a lady of mature age, and that separate seats be reserved for their use.' In the early years of the twentieth century, ladies were allowed to use the University Library if two M.A.s certified that they were seriously engaged in some branch of study, but they had to sit in a special room.

A loose system of inter-collegiate lectures began in about 1868, when five colleges decided to cover the classical tripos by making each college responsible for lectures on different subjects. By 1883 the dons of Trinity were giving weekly individual instruction to Honours students, and Trinity inaugurated the system of directors of studies, i.e. dons who supervised men's reading and gave advice.

Until 1867, no college gave a Fellowship to a scientist, and there was little teaching in scientific subjects. G. D. Liveing had fitted up a chemical laboratory in Slaughter House Lane at his own expense, and St John's later built a laboratory for him behind New Court; this existed until 1914. He became Professor of Chemistry in 1861.

A building for the natural sciences was erected in 1864-5, but there was no accommodation for experimental physics until the seventh Duke of Devonshire provided funds to erect the Cavendish Laboratory in

1872-3. James Clerk Maxwell became Professor of Experimental Physics in 1871, but for the first six years there were never more than 20 students; by 1885 there were about 100. They had to design and make their own apparatus, and the next professor, Lord Rayleigh, established a workshop and engaged a skilled mechanic who had been a Liverpool shipwright.

James Stuart, the first Professor of Mechanism and Applied Mechanics in 1875, erected workshops in Free School Lane. The machinery and equipment belonging to him was bought by the university in 1886. His successor in 1900, J. A. Ewing, persuaded the university to allow him to use the old Perse School building, and an appeal for money allowed a roof to be erected over the former yard, and for two wings to be added. The removal of the Botanic Garden provided sites for a new chemical laboratory in 1889, and an anatomy school in 1891. Five years later, the garden of Mortlock's bank was purchased, the large Examination Hall opened in 1909, and the Arts School in Bene't Street in 1911.

Downing originally possessed almost all of the ground bounded by Downing Street, Tennis Court Road, Lensfield Road, and Regent Street, an area larger than that of any other college, yet had the smallest number of students and inadequate endowments. Eight acres of these grounds were sold to the university, and in the first decade of the twentieth century many new buildings were erected on this side of Downing Street – the Sedgwick Museum of Geology, a Law School and library, the Museum of Archaeology and Ethnology, and buildings for agriculture, botany, and physiology.

J. J. Thomson followed Lord Rayleigh at the Cavendish Laboratory. He became a professor when only 28, and worked at the laboratory for 34 years, where he discovered the electron. Ernest Rutherford arrived from New Zealand in 1895, was appointed to a professorship at McGill University in 1898, and returned to Cambridge when Thomson became Master of Trinity in 1918. At the Cavendish he carried out the experiments opening up the vast new field of nuclear physics.

In the 'eighties, most of the instruments needed for medical science had to be imported from Germany, and Sir Michael Foster, Professor of Physiology, and two former pupils, Dew Smith and Francis Balfour, began to design and manufacture them. Dew-Smith took a small house in St Tibb's Row and engaged a skilful mechanic, W. T. Pye. The workshop was very successful. When more elaborate apparatus was needed, they enlisted the aid of Sir Horace Darwin. Thus began the Cambridge Scientific Instrument Co. which moved later to Chesterton Road and now occupies a large site near the railway station.

W. G. Pye, son of W. T., worked in his early years with J. J. Thomson, Lord Rutherford, and Dr G. F. Searle at the Cavendish Laboratory, and in 1896 set up business on his own account to make scientific instruments. His father joined him in partnership, and they took over Dolby's boat-building premises in Mill Lane, later moving to Chesterton. About 25 years after the foundation of the firm, they began to make wireless sets, and the well-known radio and television firm of Pye was developed. It makes a wide range of scientific instruments, broadcasting networks, radio telephones, etc., and employs about 7,000 persons in the Cambridge area, and many more in factories elsewhere. With annual sales of about £200 million, it has grown to one of the country's largest industrial concerns.

*   *   *

From 1874, considerable changes were made at Pembroke. The east and south ranges of what had been the smallest court in the university were demolished, and Waterhouse built a new Hall, Library, and a range of chambers.

The best-known don of the second half of the nineteenth century was Oscar Browning, who became a Fellow of King's in 1875. Everyone knew the man with the corpulent body on short legs, massive head, hearty manner, and deep voice. He was a strange mixture of flashes of genius, earnestness, vitality and enthusiasm, with an element of absurdity that made him a 'character'. He did not attain a high academic post, but made King's the best college for the teaching of history. He was a strong advocate of better training for teachers, and after 16 years of effort a Day Training College was established and he became the Principal at a salary of £10 a year.

He was popular with the undergraduates because he was genial and hospitable at a time when so many of the seniors remained cool and aloof. He was President of the University Bicycle Club and was the first Englishman to cross the Alps on a tricycle. He wrote that 'My tricycle was an old-fashioned type, with a carriage seat, solid tyres, and back-steering wheel moved by a handle which was worked by the right hand. With the machine I rode 961 miles – an average of 30 miles a day – and arrived at Venice with the tyres hanging in festoons.'

He was also President of the Footlights theatrical club, an officer of the Swimming, Musical, and Hockey clubs, and for 20 years Treasurer of the Union. Almost every distinguished visitor to Cambridge called on him, and among his friends were Ruskin, George Eliot, Walter Pater, and Arthur Sullivan. Princess (later Queen) Mary wrote to tell him that she would be visiting Cambridge with her brother, and would like to lunch with him. After the meal they drove round the town in a carriage.

The daily routine of Sir Donald Macalister, who came up to St John's in 1873, was no doubt typical of a 'reading man'. In his first term he rose at 6.30 a.m. to go to morning chapel at 7, finding the compulsory services tedious and dreary. He breakfasted at 7.30, then went to lectures from 8 to 9 and 11 to 12. From 1.15 to 2.15 he visited a private coach, and in the afternoons walked until dinner at 4.30. From 5.30 until 7 he wrote or read, had a cup of tea, and then studied for 3 to 4 hours. He could not afford to join any clubs, but in his second year bought a penny-farthing bicycle.

Professor G. M. Trevelyan records in his *Autobiography of an Historian* that he often walked 30 or 40 miles in a day, and once walked with Geoffrey Winthrop Young from Trinity to Marble Arch in $12\frac{3}{4}$ hours. On a hot day in 1903 Leslie Stephen walked 50 miles from Cambridge to London in 12 hours to dine with the Alpine Club. On another occasion the vicar of Eaton Socon said that his parish had been invaded by four lunatics, but was told that they were clergymen from Cambridge who had walked from Bedford. 'We left a post marked "Cambridge 30 miles" at 11.30 and reached the back gates of St. John's College at 6 p.m. We were dressed in our ordinary clothes and stopped at St. Neot's for 43 minutes.'

In the early 1880's, students wore Billycock hats, a kind of hard felt bowler, in winter, and straw hats with a band of ribbon in the college colours in summer. Straw hats were so popular at one time that it was said that more were sold and worn than in any other town of comparable size. Known elsewhere as Cambridge Boaters, or Varsity Boaters, Kelly's *Directory* for 1850 lists 11 shops making a speciality of straw hats, and

12 actual makers.

Selwyn was opened in 1882 for Church of England men of moderate means, and did not become classed as a full college until 1926.

*   *   *

The Cambridge Street Tramways Company was formed in 1878, and an Act of 1879 authorised lines from the railway station to Christ's, and to Senate House Hill. The Act was extended in 1880 to permit a line from Hyde Park Corner, along East Road to Fitzroy Street, and another short section from the Senate House to the market. Services began in 1880 on what was mainly a single track, with passing places at the University Arms Hotel, near Addenbrooke's Hospital, and Gonville Place. There was a double track from the Roman Catholic Church to the top of Station Road. A depot built in East Road accommodated eight cars and stabling for 30 horses.

The company commenced with two open-top double-deckers and four saloons. Two more double-deckers were acquired later, and two of the saloons converted to double-deckers. Along St. Andrew's Street there was a tram every few minutes, but from Market Hill only every 20 minutes. The trams moved so slowly that active persons could reach their destination more quickly by walking, and there was no need for them to stop to pick up passengers, as people could easily step on while they were in motion. The fare from the town centre to the station was 2d.

A reader of the *Chronicle* wrote in September 1882 that as an old Cantab visiting his Alma Mater after an interval of more than 40 years, he was much distressed to see how on Saturdays the trams were overladen, and the one poor horse made to draw a load which required two. People could request the trams to stop at any point, and critics pointed out that the constant stops and starts put a great deal of strain upon the horses.

Throughout the years in which the trams operated, there were frequent letters in the press alleging maltreatment of the horses, though an R.S.P.C.A. investigation showed that they were not overworked and were well cared for. On market days, standing passengers crowded on to the platform in defiance of the bylaws, people clung to the sides of the trams and even climbed on to the roof of the single-deckers. To demonstrate that the horses could easily pull even an overloaded vehicle, the company arranged an experiment in which two men pulled a car with 57 passengers from the station to the terminus opposite Christ's College without difficulty, making five short stops on the journey.

There were frequent complaints that the conductors often turned a blind eye to persons waiting to board, and the trams were said to be very noisy and dirty. Because much of the line was a single track, and cars going towards the station had to wait at the University Arms Hotel and in Station Road for one travelling in the opposite direction, people alleged that the delays had caused them to miss their trains.

For many years the only competitor of the trams was the Lion Hotel horse bus which met visitors and commercial travellers at the station. Trunks and bags containing samples were wheeled to the central shops on handcarts.

*   *   *

Market Street was widened in 1886. The Board of the Cambridge Improvement Commissioners was responsible for paving, drainage, lighting, infectious diseases, sewage disposal, and all sanitary matters, also plans for new buildings. When the Board was abolished in 1889, the Town Council decided to give serious consideration to the question of sewage, and raised a loan of £150,000 to build new sewers and a sewage farm at Milton Road.

W. E. Heitland, who came up in 1867, wrote in *After Many Years* that when the town was sewered 'the stench from the man-hole of the new sewer was horrible, and further outlay for ventilation needed. In my younger days it was a common undergraduate saying that the Cam was only kept going by the Town sewerage'. The *Chronicle* reported on 6 September 1873, that water had been drawn off 'for the removal of the pestilential contents of the channel near the Great Bridge known as Bin Brook, it being especially filthy where the college privies empty direct into the river. These and those between Newnham Mill and Barnwell pool are a constant source of pollutions, and will be a great expense as long as the dredger has periodically to be used'.

The *Cambridge Independent Press* of 18 October 1873, stated that 19 main outfalls of sewers discharged into the river between Magdalene

Bridge and Barnwell Pool. Between Jesus Sluice and Baitsbite Lock, nearly four miles, the river was little better than a huge cesspool, receiving the sewerage of about 30,000 persons. During recent town boat races, the screw-propelled pleasure boat, the *Alma Mater,* plying up and down the river, created a serious nuisance.

Likewise, the *Cambridge Review* of June 1888, said that 'One afternoon as we were coming up the river we met a steam barge going down, and the stench that arose from the bottom of the river was as bad, if not worse, than that of stale fish in a seaport town in summer. It seems a wonder that more boating men are not laid up with typhoid fever.'

The County Council was formed in accordance with the Local Government Act of 1888, and took over responsibility for the Quarter Sessions and the maintenance of main roads.

In 1884 the Town Council agreed to purchase Christ's Pieces from Jesus College for £500, and to spend no less than £500 in draining, levelling and planting. The Free Library gained an additional building at the corner of Peas Hill, and the *Chronicle* reported that 'Since the new room was opened there has been a large number of lady readers and the Committee have ordered that a separate table be set apart for their use.' A new bridge over the Little New River at the end of Bateman Street was opened, and in 1885 the Roman Catholic Church was built with funds provided by Mrs Lyne-Stephens, a French lady who was the most famous Victorian ballet dancer in London. A large new Cattle Market was laid out at the corner of Cherryhinton Road, whither on market days herds of cattle were driven through the streets, and in some places railings were erected beside the footpaths to protect the public.

The first march of the Salvation Army took place in June 1885. The procession was headed by a brass band, and accompanied by a crowd, mostly members of the rowdy class. Some of the ruffians attacked the Salvationists, and many were knocked down. While passing Maid's Causeway, some of the crowd pelted them with sods and mud from the Common. The most serious incident occurred in Burleigh Street, where the crowd broke the ranks of the bandsmen and smashed both ends of the big drum. While the Salvationists were meeting in Sturton Town Hall, a large and unruly crowd shouted outside.

Three days later there was such a great disturbance in the Hall that a hose was turned on the people at the back. In the early days of the Army, women joined in attacks on the members, pulling bonnets from the heads of girls and trampling them underfoot. During meetings held on Parker's Piece on Sunday afternoons, the crowd sometimes seized the bandsmen's instruments and kicked them round like footballs. Many of the Salvationists had their clothes torn and uniforms ruined.

A disused skating rink in St Andrew's Street was opened in 1882 as a theatre called St Andrew's Hall, changing its name later to The Theatre Royal, by W. B. Redfern and J. W. Clark, who became the University Registrary. A local newspaper said that 'The thanks of both Town and University are due to Mr. Redfern for founding this establishment and keeping it free from the faintest approach of objectionable accompaniment.' Master Charles Chaplin and his brother Sidney appeared in *Sherlock Holmes* on this stage. The New Theatre was built in 1895, and opened in January 1896 with the Haymarket Theatre Co. headed by Mr (later Sir Herbert) Beerbohm Tree in *Hamlet.* Gerald du Maurier was also in the cast. In 1899 the Rodney Cricket Club gave a concert and dramatic performance which was so successful that a dramatic committee was formed to establish the Rodney Dramatic Club.

The tripos examinations had been opened to women in 1881, but amid scenes of great excitement, the Council of the Senate rejected proposals that they should be given degrees in 1888 and 1896-97. The *Cambridge Review* organized a poll to test the opinion of undergraduates, and 1,723 were opposed to degrees for women, only 446 being in favour.

The building of many houses on the De Freville Estate made it necessary to provide a more direct route between the centre of the town and Chesterton across Midsummer Common, and although this was rough and little used except for grazing, there were many who opposed the scheme. The advocates of the project prevailed, and the foundation stone of Victoria Bridge was laid in 1889. The Cam Bridges Act sanctioned a second bridge which was not built until 1970.

By an Act of 1889 the university and the town began to co-operate in local government. The Senate appointed two councillors and four others were elected by the colleges. This was later altered to allow the university to choose two aldermen and six councillors, and this arrangement persisted until the reorganisation of local government in 1974.

In 1888-93 the finances of the colleges and the university were severely strained, and colleges were unable to pay their full contributions for university purposes. They derived most of their income from the ownership of land, and were gravely affected by the depression in agriculture. Unfortunately, this was at a time when there was an urgent need for additional laboratories and lecture rooms, also more lecturers in both the older and the newer subjects. A Cambridge University Association was formed in 1898 to attempt to induce wealthy men to offer benefactions.

May Week Balls did not begin until the 1890's. Students still wore caps and gowns, even when walking in the country on Sundays. Pictures of boats on the river show men wearing bowler hats, black coats, and stiff collars. It was not until after 1910 that most undergraduates began to discard hats. Patent leather shoes were popular from 1900-10.

Many 'reading parties' were organized during the early part of the twentieth century, when dons would rent a furnished house at the seaside or in the country during the Long Vacation, and take a number of undergraduates to study under their supervision.

More lower middle class boys and a few from working class families came to Cambridge with the assistance of local authorities when an Act of 1891 allowed county councils to award scholarships. Poor boys could pay their way by gaining school-leaving exhibitions, university prizes and college scholarships. One who did so was Sir Ernest Barker, who gained his degree at Oxford but became a well-known Cambridge don. His father was a farm and quarry labourer and his mother had worked in a cotton mill. He gained a scholarship to Manchester Grammar School and a master taught him Greek without payment. He was able to go to Balliol in 1893 with a scholarship and leaving exhibition, and twice won the Craven. With an interest-free loan from his mother's grocer, he had just enough money, although he had to go without his Hall dinners on two or three nights a week.

On 28 May 1890 a crowd gathered outside the Senate House to hear three dons read the names of those who had gained Honours in the Mathematical Tripos. First came the names of the successful men, then a don announced 'Women' and they raised their caps, the men in the crowd doing likewise. As was customary, two or three men cried 'Ladies, sir, ladies,' at which the don repeated 'Women'. There was some applause for the name of Miss P. G. Fawcett, but it was not until a week later that it became known that she had been placed above the Senior Wrangler. A party of undergraduates then went to Newnham to serenade her, commencing with 'Only one whisper, one,' and ending with 'Queen of my Heart'.

'W.F.R.' writing of *Cambridge in 1891,* says: 'In 1891 beyond all doubt the mainspring of the University was the Collegiate system. The undergraduates, far more homogeneous than now (1943), ate, worshipped, received instruction and for the most part lived within the walls of jealous and mutually aggressive institutions ... Whatever compulsory Chapel failed to do, it gave men a common topic ... There was far more obvious interest in Theology. A Professor has described the men's midnight tramping of the court to discuss the University Sermon ... A rowing man who applied for some dispensation during Lent was told that a sardine at breakfast might be permissable.'

'The University was still small and outstanding personalities were widely known by sight ... Hats and often gloves would be worn at a football match. Stiff white shirts and collars were normal, and only men from Scottish schools dispensed with a football cap. In at least one College it was bad form to appear on King's Parade in games clothes'.

There were about 30 brewers and 250 publicans in the town. In 1891 it was announced that the University Press was prosperous and was going to extend, as work could be found for three or four more printing machines. A building would be erected in Silver Street on the site occupied by Dring, a noted sausage-maker. The noise of the Press machines nearby was often mistaken for the machines that made this famous Cambridge commodity.

Peterhouse, the oldest college, was the first to be lighted throughout by electricity, on the Ferranti system, under the supervision of Sir William Thompson, a Fellow. Baily, Grundy and Barrett generated electricity at 2 St Mary's Passage with a gas engine and a dynamo. For the first two years current was supplied only for lighting during the hours of darkness, but as the demand increased, a continuous 24-hour supply was provided. The company sold the goodwill of their business as electricity suppliers to the Cambridge Electric Supply Co. in 1896.

Trinity introduced electricity in 1893, and in 1894 it was said that the Hall and Chapel of Emmanuel were now lighted by electric light on the Edison and Swan system, and that if it proved successful, the whole college would be so lighted.

ELEVEN

The Twentieth Century, 1890-1950

The Proctors still possessed powers to arrest women 'suspected of evil', although under the law of the land a prostitute could only be arrested if guilty of solicitation. On 11 February 1891 Jane Elsden was arrested and imprisoned in the Spinning House, but escaped and went to her father's house at Dullingham. The Vice-Chancellor unwisely caused her to be re-arrested, which meant that she would have to be tried in public on a charge of breaking prison. London newspapers referred to 'An Academic Star Chamber,' Labouchere asked a question in the House of Commons, and the Home Secretary issued an order for her release.

The Borough Council resented these arbitrary powers possessed by the university, and there were long negotiations between the two parties about prostitutes. It was agreed that in future, Spinning House proceedings would be heard in public, and that accused women could receive professional assistance. On 3 December 1891, a Proctor arrested Daisy Hopkins, who was walking with a member of the university, and she was sentenced to 14 days imprisonment. An application was made to the High Court for a writ of Habeas Corpus, and the Lord Chief Justice ordered her release.

Acrimonious negotiations between the university and the Council dragged on for three years, until the parties combined to promote The Cambridge University and Corporation Act of 1894 which retained the Proctors' powers of arrest, but stipulated that offending persons would be taken to the Police Station and in due course appear before the Borough Bench of Magistrates. Under the same Act, the Vice-Chancellor lost his power to license stage-plays.

On the day after the concluding day of the May Races there was always a boat procession. The eights, one from each college, decorated with flowers and laurel leaves, and with college flags flying, assembled at the Mill Pool and then rowed to King's, where huge crowds, sometimes numbering 10,000, stood on the lawn. The crews wore bright blazers and straw hats decorated with ribbons and flowers.

The boats were ranged side by side across the river, and the crew of the second boat called for three cheers for the Head of the River crew, who then drank seated while all the other crews stood with uplifted oars and cheered them. This process was repeated until all of the crews had been toasted. James, in *Eton and King's,* says that 'In the boats, cups filled with alcoholic drinks passed from hand to hand, and most of them found a night's lodging in the river bed, whence they were dredged up next day by the employees of Mr Miller, from whom they were hired. We of King's rather resented the incursion of the Town over our lawn, and used to watch them with some dislike.'

The last boat procession was held in 1892, when 30 boats, rowing in two divisions, had competed. The Lady Margaret boat was manned by only three men dressed in mourning instead of their club colour of bright scarlet, and in the places of the missing men were placards reading SENT DOWN. They had been ordered to leave the university for taking part in a bonfire in New Court on the previous night.

The *Cambridge Review* of 8 June 1893 reported that 'It has finally been decided that there shall be no Boat Procession this year ... The show had lost all interest since the regular crews had ceased to take part in it, and it involved a useless expenditure which most clubs, we fancy, will be glad to be spared.' Many people, however, no doubt regretted the passing of these spectacles, and that for one day in the year they could tread on the sacred lawn.

*   *   *

Skating was a favourite sport, and the champions of England were usually Fenmen until a number of indoor rinks were built in other parts of the country and they were faced by competitors who could practise throughout the year. In 1895 there was a great frost from January until March, and for two months it was possible to skate on the river to Ely and beyond. No football matches were played for three months, and the university soccer club were not able to hold a trial match until just before they met Oxford.

Electric lights installed at three fields at the Newnham end of Grantchester Meadows enabled skaters to flock there in the evenings, and there were ice carnivals with people in costume, and a band to provide music. A race held on the river from Bottisham Lock to Ely, back to Bottisham and then to Ely again, a distance of $37\frac{1}{2}$ miles, resulted in a dead heat between A. E. Tebbit and H. A. Palmer, the leading amateur skaters of the time. Just before a thaw set in, two men skated from Cambridge to Denver Sluice and back to Clayhithe, covering 72 miles.

*   *   *

A recent proposal for a new road across Coe Fen and the Lammas Land to Barton Road evoked numerous protests, but in 1895 there was a scheme for a road on a viaduct so that the trams could go down Bateman Street and continue to the corner of Barton Road. A correspondent of the *Cambridge Chronicle* wrote that this road would attract 'the people from the slums and alleys of our congested, unhealthy town into the green lanes and fair meadow land of the country where the wild violet blows and the daffodil dances in the breeze and the winter aconite hangs its golden bell'. In spite of this lyrical effusion, nothing came of the scheme.

In 1896 the Tramways Company was alarmed to learn that an Omnibus Company had applied for a licence to operate eight two-horse omnibuses at a fare of 1d. from the station to the centre of the town, and 1d. from the centre to various points in the suburbs. The tram fare was 2d., and the omnibuses would of course travel more speedily. When it became clear that the Corporation and the public welcomed this scheme, the Tramways Company hastily bought four single-deck one-horse omnibuses, and had two of them on the road three months before the new company began operations.

The *Chronicle* reported in May 1896 that 'Considerable interest was created amongst the townspeople on Wednesday, when the Cambridge Omnibus Company began to run their new and convenient two-horse omnibuses from the railway station to the Market Hill. The four vehicles embody all the latest improvements, and have a seating capacity of 12 inside and 14 outside, the exterior accommodation being seven comfortable garden seats.'

There was insufficient demand for two companies running over the same routes, and sometimes two competing vehicles came along at almost the same time, both without a single passenger. The receipts of the Tramways Company fell drastically, but surprisingly it was the Omnibus Company which, after four years of competition, offered to abandon the routes served by the trams if the Tramway Company would withdraw their omnibuses serving the suburbs. The Omnibus Company bought their vehicles, but in spite of the elimination of competition, passengers were few in number, and in 1902 the company ceased to operate. In 1899 and 1904 there were abortive proposals for an electric tram system.

The Hon. C. S. Rolls rode a motorcycle in the Corn Exchange in 1898, and he owned the first car seen in Cambridge, a 5 h.p. Peugeot. The second belonged to Dr Arthur Cook and the third to Professor Inglis. Rolls was said to be the most daring of the Trinity nocturnal roof-climbers who published *The Roof-Climbers' Guide to Trinity College*. He was also the first man to fly from England to France and back.

W. King and H. H. Harper, who had a small cycle repair shop in Sussex Street, had their first motor ride when they travelled to Ely on a De Dion tricycle with a trailer which Rolls had brought over from France, with a French mechanic. The firm began to build motor tricycles and bicycles, and in 1900 a four-wheeler. In 1902 they were awarded a gold medal at the Crystal Palace Exhibition, and in 1904 King won the Motor Cycling Club competition on his 'King' machine. The firm eventually decided to concentrate on the sale and repair of motor vehicles had they decided to continue to manufacture them, as did Morris at Oxford, Cambridge would no doubt be a very different city today.

*   *   *

An article in *The Idler* in 1898 said that 'If an undergraduate of the last century could revisit Cambridge now, he would find his University so changed that he would have some difficulty in recognising it. College buildings have increased twofold, and the faces of those he would have known have in many cases been altered. There are pavements and lamp-posts, trams and bicycles, a Roman Catholic "Cathedral." and

Opposite top: *The river opposite King's College, showing barges towed by horse walking in the river*
Opposite bottom: *The Boat Procession in Honour of the Prince and Princess of Wales, 1864, from* **The Illustrated London News**

Cambridge Tram.
Decored Feb 18 1915

heatre, ladies' colleges and married dons, each with his villa and his
erambulator, past, present, or potential.'

Lord Kitchener received an honorary degree on the afternoon of 24
November 1898. He drove from Christ's to the Senate House, where an
mmense crowd was waiting. Some people climbed the railings, and a
ortion gave way while he was in the Senate House. When he left, the
orses were taken out of his carriage and he was drawn to Christ's Lodge,
vhile mounted police were quite unable to control the vast crowd. In the
Court, his carriage, somewhat damaged, was surrounded by people
vishing to shake his hand, and he had great difficulty in reaching the
Lodge. There were calls for a speech, and he began 'Gentlemen, you have
1ade it hotter for me here than I ever found it in the Sudan.'

He had been due to visit the Union, where another crowd awaited
im, but his new uniform had been damaged, and it seemed unwise to
enture out. His cousin, Mrs Peile, suggested that he should change into
ivilian clothes and go there by side streets. In the evening, Masters and
rofessors dined with him at Christ's, while undergraduates had a huge
onfire on Market Hill which burned until midnight. The whole town
vas scoured for wood to feed the flames, and railings, shutters from shop
vindows, and even the doors of houses were stolen.

The notorious Spinning House was demolished in 1901, and a Police
tation and Fire Brigade Station arose on the site. The Town Council
ecame responsible for elementary education in 1902 when the Education
ct abolished school boards. In the old schools, parents had paid between
d and 9d. a week for each child, unless they were too poor. Secondary
chools became the responsibility of the County Council.

At the beginning of the century, many people lived over their shops in
etty Cury, Market Street and Sidney Street. On Sundays they all went
 church, the men in top hats, frock coats and striped trousers; the ladies
 silks and satins. In courts behind the main thoroughfares, and
rticularly in King Street and Newmarket Road, lived large numbers of
oor workers who never went to church because their clothes were too
abby.

Realising this, Canon Proctor of Holy Trinity Church had pamphlets
nnouncing special men's services delivered to every house in the parish.
xty men came to the first service, 300 to the second. A thousand cards
ere left at works and offices each month, and distributed at football

matches on Parker's Piece. The ordinary morning service then lasted until 1.15, and after a time the church was left open after the worshippers had departed. By 1.30 the building was again crowded with men, some eating their lunch. Before long the congregations completely filled the church, and the Henry Martyn Hall had to be used as well.

The population increased from 9,276 in 1801 to 38,379 a century later. If one included Chesterton and other districts which geographically formed part of Cambridge, the population in 1905 was in excess of 53,000, i.e. five times as large as a hundred years earlier. The new part of the town had grown up along and adjoining the old country roads creating an unplanned network of small streets. Narrow passages often gave access to rows of cottages between these streets.

In 1906, in England and Wales, there was one public-house for every 230 persons; in Cambridge there was one for every 138. In Newmarket Road there were 22 public-houses in a distance of 796 yards, and between the foot of Castle Hill and the corner of Histon Road, a distance of 510 yards, there were 10. Barnwell, Castle End and parts of New Town had many prostitutes. The latter was originally called New Zealand, and when Coronation Street was built at the time of the coronation of George IV, the postal address was Coronation Street, New Zealand.

The coronation of Edward VII was celebrated in 1902 by a procession designed to illustrate progress in national and local affairs. It was divided into five sections to demonstrate municipal, imperial and social progress; locomotion and physical culture; and trade exhibits. It was headed by the Town Council and officials, followed by the Volunteer Fire Brigade, the Suffolk Imperial Yeomanry, the Friendly Societies, a wagonette of soccer players, and a group of athletes from the Albert Institute. There was the customary balloon ascent from Parker's Piece, and afternoon and evening fireworks.

An important group of new university buildings, the Sedgwick Museum of Geology, the Squire Law Library, Law School, and Botany School were opened in 1904 by Edward VII and Queen Alexandra. These were the first buildings put up on the south side of Downing Street.

A *Cambridge Chronicle* report in that year complained about the entire absence of any order on the river during the May Races, and the number of accidents that occurred in consequence. 'A more haphazard ar-

disorderly scene can hardly be imagined, than was presented each night of the "Mays" at the conclusion of the racing. Steam launches, panting, wheezing, and hooting like asthmatical motor cars, huge barges fitted up as houseboats and drawn by horses, ferry boats with their dangerous chains and innumerable small craft were all trying to make their way along the river at one and the same time and with an absence of order that could only end in disaster.'

A tragedy did occur on the concluding day of the races in the following year. A heavily-laden ferry had just pulled away from the Ditton bank, when two undergraduates jumped aboard, causing the boat to capsize. More than twenty people were thrown into the river, and although there were many boats close at hand, three young women were drowned because their clothing became entangled with the chain of the ferry.

The *Students' Handbook* of 1902 claimed that college and intercollegiate teaching was adequate, and that there was no longer any need for most undergraduates to have private tuition. When the order of merit in the Mathematical Tripos was abolished in 1907, coaching finally became unnecessary.

Between 1902 and 1907 Emmanuel College proposed that Emmanuel Street should be closed, but negotiations with the Corporation broke down, and when North Court, completed in 1914, was built, an underground tunnel was made.

*   *   *

The Cambridge Light Blue Company began to operate motor buses in April, 1905, and a rival company, the Cambridge Motor Bus Co. soon appeared. The 'Light Blues' only ran for six months because they did not pay, also a conductor had died after he had put his head out and struck something, involving the company in high legal costs. The other company also experienced difficulties; it was fined because one of its buses was found guilty of 'not consuming its own smoke', and in 1906 the Corporation revoked its licence after there had been a number of minor accidents, such as knocking down lamp-posts.

In 1907, J. B. Walford was granted a licence for his green 'Ortona' buses. While living in Egham, Surrey, he had manufactured a motorcycle,

so-called, and had traded as the Ortona Motor Co., the name being taken
from a P. and O. steamer list. He purchased the Cambridge Motor
Omnibus Co., change the name to Ortona, and obtained a licence for
three single- and one double-deck bus. The Ortona Motor Co. Ltd was
registered as a limited company in 1908.

He gradually increased the number of vehicles, but for a time the
double-deckers were not permitted in the central streets because it was
thought that they might damage shop blinds and signs. So many
passengers forsook the slower trams that by 1912 the company was
scarcely solvent. In January 1914 a winding-up order was made at the
instigation of the Borough Council because the company owed road
charges. In 1913 the Ortona Co. arranged a partnership with the British
Automobile Co. Ltd.

Women became eligible to become County or Borough Councillors in
1907, provided that they were householders. This meant that they had to
be either widows or spinsters. When an Act of 1914 enabled the wife of
a householder to stand for election, Cambridge was the first town to
make use of the Act.

Cambridge people first saw moving pictures in large tents at the
Midsummer Fair. Taylor's 'Coliseum de Luxe' announced that it had
1,700 plush lounge seats, and Thurston's urged the public to visit their
'Electric Vaudeville' to see 'this wonder which may never occur again, as
it is booked up for all the principal towns of Great Britain and the
Continent'. In 1910 the chief attraction was pictures of the funeral of
Edward VII, and when pictures of workers leaving the University Press
were shown, people were excited to recognise acquaintances. Travelling
shows, 'Animated Photographs,' 'Electric Life Motion Pictures,' and
'The Bioscope' visited the town at other times.

The Corporation obtained a cinematograph licence for the Guildhall
and the Corn Exchange in March 1910, and in the same year licences
were granted to Sturton Town Hall (called at first the Empire and now
the Kinema). The latter was a music-hall until 1914, and then for two
years combined variety with films. From 1908 A. J. Pointer had
occasionally used the Alexandra Hall of the Y.M.C.A. for cinema shows
and in 1910 he converted the Victoria Assembly Room on Market Hill
into the first Cambridge cinema. He had previously used the building as a
skating-rink. He converted the Empire into a picture palace in 1916.

The first building to be erected as a cinema was the Playhouse in Mill Road in 1913. The Rendezvous opened in Magrath Avenue in 1915, but was destroyed by fire, and the Rex replaced it on the same site in 1932. There was no large cinema in the centre of the town until the Central opened in 1921. Rebuilt in 1928, in 1929 it showed the first talkies, *The Broadway Melody* and *Show Boat*. The Tivoli in Chesterton Road arrived in 1925, and the old Victoria closed a year later to enable the new Victoria to open in 1931. The Cosmopolitan (now the Arts) began in 1933, and in the same year the New Theatre became a cinema. Finally, in 1937, the Regal was built on the site of the old Castle Hotel which had been severely damaged in a fire.

The first man to land an aeroplane in Cambridge, in 1911, was Sub. Lieut W. B. Rhodes Moorhouse, an undergraduate. People on Parker's Piece were astounded when he brought down his Blériot monoplane, and he later used it to travel between the town and his home in Huntingdon. During the war of 1914-18 he was awarded the Victoria Cross for most conspicuous gallantry as an officer of the Royal Flying Corps, and died later of wounds received in action.

Army manoeuvres were held in the vicinity of Cambridge in 1912, attended by King George V, who stayed at Trinity, and a sentry-box was erected outside the Great Gate. The boundaries of the Borough were extended in 1911 to include most of Chesterton and parts of the parishes of Grantchester, Trumpington and Cherryhinton.

The outbreak of the war in 1914 severely curtailed the work of the university, and at the beginning of the Michaelmas Term only 1,700 of the normal 3,600 undergraduates were in residence. The Sixth Division under General Plumer assembled at Cambridge, and thousands of soldiers encamped on the commons or were billeted all over the town. The Division landed in France on the 8 September. The First Eastern General Hospital was set up under the cloisters of Nevile's Court and in marquees erected on the lawns of Trinity, until hutted accommodation was provided on the King's and Clare Cricket Ground in Burrell's Walk, now the site of the University Library. About 2,000 officer cadets were quartered in the colleges, and by 1916 only 575 students were in residence.

After the war, state scholarships and grants to ex-service men raised the number of undergraduates to 5,733 by 1920. The finances of the university were severely strained, and many thought that only a grant from the Government would solve the problem. Others opposed this, fearing that the university would lose its autonomy. The first grant from public funds was made in 1919-20.

A Royal Commission to consider the universities of Oxford and Cambridge was appointed in 1919. It proposed that fees for courses should be paid to Faculty Boards instead of to the colleges or to individual lecturers; that there should be a retiring age and a pensions scheme for professors and lecturers; that half of the Fellowships should be held by university lecturers and demonstrators; that legislative power should be transferred from the Senate to the Regent House; and that the scale of contributions made by the colleges to the university should vary according to their wealth.

A pension scheme was adopted in 1923, and a Statutory Commission of 1923-5 approved most of the proposals made by the Royal Commission. New statutes which came into force in 1926 enabled women to become professors or lecturers, and a centralised secretariat was established.

Before the First World War there were few multiple shops in Cambridge, though Boots, Freeman, Hardy and Willis, the International, Lipton's, the Maypole Dairy, and Peark's had already arrived, and some have since disappeared. Between the two wars, the rebuilding of the whole of the block from Sussex Street to Lloyd's Bank provided sites for the Dorothy Café and Ballroom, Heffer's stationery shop, Woolworth, and Marks and Spencer.

When an Act of 1919 allowed women to become magistrates, Cambridge had a larger number than any other Borough when the Lord Chancellor issued the first list in 1920. The Volunteer Fire Brigade held its last parade in January 1921, when its duties were taken over by the police.

In politics, the 1920's saw the early days of the Labour Party, and their first candidate, the Rev. Rhonda Williams, a man of strong pacifist and temperance views, did not, to the surprise of some people, lose his deposit in a parliamentary election. The first seat on the Town Council was won in Romsey ward, where there were many railway workers, followed by gains in Abbey and St Matthew's. One of the successful candidates was Mrs Clara Rackham, the wife of a don. Albert Stubbs, a printer, and later organiser for the Transport and General Workers' Union, became a town and county councillor, and in 1945 was elected M.P. for Cambridgeshire after a campaign in the villages, which he toured on his motorcycle.

In 1921 the Council of the Senate agreed that women should be given the titles of degrees, and a crowd of undergraduates went to Newnham College and damaged the bronze gates erected to commemorate the first Mistress. In 1926 women became eligible to become members of faculties and faculty boards and could fill any teaching post. Undergraduates began to dress more informally in flannels and tweed sports jackets, although starched white shirts were worn at the Amateur Dramatic Club theatre and in the stalls of the New Theatre. Caps and gowns were always worn at lectures and after sunset. At this period there were many hoaxes and 'rags,' and the General Strike of 1926 was welcomed by some of the junior members of the university because it occurred just before the tripos examinations were due; lectures were suspended and the examinations postponed, and many undergraduates undertook work in maintaining essential services.

In the same year Terence Gray re-opened the old Theatre Royal in Newmarket Road as the Festival Theatre, installed a new stage with a turntable, and the first cyclorama in the country. There were a number of excitingly experimental productions, and his company included Ninette de Valois and Maurice Evans, who became a well-known Shakespearean actor in the U.S.A. Alistair Cooke was theatre critic of the undergraduate journal *The Gownsman.*

Later, when A. B. Horne, calling himself Anmer Hall, took over for eighteen months, he had in his company Flora Robson and Robert Donat, with Tyrone Guthrie as producer. Terence Gray gave up the Festival in 1933, and Joseph McLeod's repertory company played there until growing competition from the cinemas forced a closure in 1935.

There was much controversy when, in 1928, the Town Council decided to widen Coe Fen Lane, bridge the river, and construct a new road across Sheep's Green, but the growth of traffic soon proved that it had been a very necessary undertaking. In the same year, conspicuous landmarks disappeared when the King's and Bishop's Mills were demolished.

In 1924, when Clare built Memorial Court, designed by Sir Giles

Gilbert Scott, it became the first of the men's colleges to build beyond Queen's Road. The funds for many new university buildings and endowments for new professorships came from commercial firms, private individuals, and other sources. The Rockefeller Foundation, for instance, provided funds for a Pathological Laboratory opened in 1928, and a new wing of the Cavendish Laboratory was built with money donated by Lord Austin.

Lord Rutherford, at the Cavendish, was not only a great scientist, but a man who inspired his staff and students, creating, it is said, 'an atmosphere that no one who experienced it will forget'. Sir John Cockcroft and E. T. S. Walton discovered the artificial disintegration of protons in 1932, and Sir James Chadwick discovered the neutron.

Peter Kapitza, the Russian scientist, arrived in Cambridge in the early 1920's and worked closely with Lord Rutherford. The Royal Society offered to build and equip a laboratory for his magnetic researches, and a gift from Dr Ludwig Mond enabled the Royal Society Mond Laboratory to open in 1932. Kapitza was a Fellow of Trinity, and might well have spent the rest of his life in Cambridge, but when he visited Moscow in 1934, the Soviet Government forbade him to return. The equipment of his laboratory was bought by the Russians, and Kapitza has since been acknowledged as the father figure of modern Russian science.

A much-needed block of lecture-rooms for the arts faculties was built in Mill Lane in 1933. By this time, nearly half of the undergraduates were in receipt of financial assistance. The appearance of the Market Square was radically changed in 1934 when all of the buildings on the northern side were replaced by a new block for Caius designed by Murray Easton. A few years later, new dignified municipal buildings arose to enlarge the Guildhall. Queens' spread across the river in 1935 when a long curved range was constructed, and the old brewhouse and stables were converted into a Common Room.

The boundaries of the town were again extended in 1934 to include the remainder of Chesterton, Cherryhinton, and Trumpington, and parts of Great Shelford, Fen Ditton, Impington, and Milton, and the population then exceeded 70,000. A row of old timber-framed houses and shops in Peas Hill was demolished in 1935 to make way for extensions to the Guildhall. It was found that one had been built in about 1450 with oak timbers from a broken-up ship, and part of the flooring vas made from the two-foot wide deck planks of a ship. Fine linen-fold panelling was discovered beneath 27 coats of paint.

Bridge Street was much changed and widened when all of the buildings on one side were pulled down for extensions to St John's, designed by Sir Edward Maufe, begun in 1938 and completed in 1942. In St Andrew's Street, Prudential House, 1957-9, and Bradwell's Court, 1960-62, replaced the former property between Christ's and Emmanuel Street.

A Rockefeller Foundation gift of £700,000 enabled the university to build a new Library and Zoological Laboratory. For a site for the University Library, the authorities wisely decided to go to the other side of the river, to the former sports ground of King's and Clare between Burrell's Walk and West Road. Here the new Library, designed by Sir Giles Gilbert Scott, was opened in 1934, and the old buildings were adapted for university reception rooms and offices. Cockerell's building was assigned to the Squire Law Library and the Seeley Historical Library.

The new Library is a large steel-framed edifice of russet brick, 420 feet long, with a massive central tower of 12 storeys rising to 160 feet. It is the third largest library in the country, and it took eight weeks to transfer the books. Although the Library had 250,000 feet of shelving, thought to be adequate for 50 years, by 1960 there was a pressing need for more space. A wing on six levels has been added to the rear of Scott's building, to provide a large increase in the amount of shelving and additional reading-rooms and workrooms.

In 1938-39 all of the buildings in Sussex Street were replaced by buildings with shops on the ground floor, designed by E. R. Barrow. On the Sidney College side the upper floors provided rooms for undergraduates.

In 1936 Lord Keynes built and gave to the town the Arts Theatre, hoping that the people of Cambridge would be able to see there the best in the five arts of drama, opera, music, ballet and cinema. The theatre was an outstanding success, and among other achievements it created for the first time in Cambridge an audience for ballet. Lady Keynes, as Lydia Lopokova, had of course been one of the most famous ballerinas of her time.

The war years favoured Cambridge theatre audiences, since restrictions

in London caused many stars who normally appeared only in th
metropolis to play at the Arts Theatre. The trustees also organisec
concerts of solo and chamber music. On Sundays, music-hall stars lik
Leslie Henson, Frances Day, Florence Desmond, Beatrice Lillie and Fre
Emney gave performances for the forces.

During the Second World War there were still many undergraduate
in residence, as some secured deferment, and about 2,000 from th
London School of Economics and Bedford College were evacuated te
Cambridge. Many dons went into the forces or the civil service. Unti
1939 most scientists at the universities had taken a somewhat detachec
view about the possible practical applications of their work, but the wa
brought a changed outlook.

Government departments occupied some of the colleges, and all of th
windows of King's College Chapel were removed for safety. There wer
a number of air-raids, but with the exception of the Union, damage tc
university and college buildings was slight, as the railway statior
appeared to be the main target. It was suggested that Hitler did not mak
large-scale raids on Cambridge because he wanted to spare Heidelberg
After the war, Heidelberg was 'twinned' with Cambridge.

With the return of peace, the number of students rose from 5,374 ir
1938-39 to 7,016 in 1954-55. In 1946, about 90% of the places wer
filled by ex-service applicants, and while national service continued, mos
of the men did not come up until after they had served. Women wer
admitted to full membership of the university in 1947, and the Queer
Mother became the first Cambridge woman graduate when she receivec
an Honorary Degree.

TWELVE

The Twentieth Century, 1950-1975

The Cambridge Development Plan prepared by Sir William Holford and Professor Myles Wright in 1950 emphasised that the city must remain predominantly a university town; that no large-scale industry should be permitted; that the population within the town map area should not exceed 100,000, although development in appropriate nearby villages could accommodate a further 7,500 persons.

To remedy traffic congestion, their main proposal was for a new 'Spine Relief Road' from the corner of Histon Road to Chesterton Road near the foot of Magrath Avenue, a bridge here, and a road skirting Jesus Green and Christ's Pieces to join St Andrew's Street at Emmanuel Street. A multi-storey car park, shops and offices were proposed for the Lion Yard site.

The authors of the plan could not foresee that Cambridge would soon be in the centre of the most rapidly growing area of the country, with a population increasing at double the rate anticipated. By 1961 the population of the county exceeded the figure that had been forecast for 1971. There has been endless controversy about the 'Spine Relief Road' proposal, and no part of it has yet been constructed. For the Lion Yard site there were several abortive plans, and it has only recently been developed for shops and offices and a new Public Library. For this scheme, all of the buildings on one side of Petty Cury were demolished.

The largest amount of new housing since 1955 has been built on the Arbury and King's Hedges Estates. The former has its own shopping centre, church, schools and public-houses, but the winding minor roads form a chaotic pattern and odd open spaces have wasted a great deal of

building land. Silver Street Bridge was rebuilt in 1959. The firs
multi-storey car park was built in 1962-68 in Park Street, followed b
others in Gonville Place and the Lion Yard. An indoor swimming poo
was constructed in Gonville Place in 1961-63, and Fire Brigad
Headquarters and Police Headquarters later, both in Parkside.

A municipal airport would not have been commercially viable, an
Cambridge is unique in having a fully-equipped airport available fo
public use, but provided by a commercial firm. The founder of Marsha
was caterer to the Pitt Club, and when students began to acquire moto
cars, he opened a garage in Jesus Lane to store and service them. The firm
has developed into a large organisation based on road and air transpor
which employs 2,500 people. It owns garages, has a military an
commercial motor-body and bus division, manufactures aircraf
components, etc. The largest civil and military aircraft can land on th
aerodrome for overhaul or maintenance, and the company designed an
manufactured the droop nose and visor for the Concorde.

In the last 20 years, there has been a prodigious amount of universit
and college building, and the academics abandoned the timid an
conventional styles of the preceding decades, and boldly employed th
foremost contemporary architects; men like Chamberlin, Dowson
Casson, Lasdun, Sheppard, Spence and Stirling. Some have produce
buildings which, though essentially modern, blend well with adjoining
older work in scale and treatment. Other major new buildings are s
original and assertive that only time will show whether they are wholl
acceptable.

The new buildings are so numerous that it is impossible to mention
them all. The Engineering Laboratory began to move to Fen Causeway
in 1948, and the first buildings have since then greatly extended. A larg
Chemical Laboratory was built in 1953-60 on a rather cramped site in
Lensfield Road at a cost of £2.25 million, and a Veterinary School was
opened in 1955 in Madingley Road. The university purchased
Madingley Hall, where Edward VII had resided when he was an
undergraduate, to serve as a residence for research students.

Work began in 1956 on a major scheme for the arts faculties on the
former Corpus playing fields in Sidgwick Avenue, designed by Sir Hugh
Casson and Neville Conder. There is a tall block of ten lecture theatres
seating a total of 950 people, another building contains the libraries and

rooms for the faculties of medieval and modern languages, English, and moral sciences; others house economics and politics and oriental studies. There are also the Lady Mitchell Hall seating 450 and the Little Hall seating 150.

On this site there is also James Stirling's History Faculty building (1964-68), one of the most striking modern buildings in Cambridge and, internally at least, a great architectural work. Two wings of an L-shaped faculty block enclose a tent-shaped roof of glass over the library.

The original plan of 1961 by Denys Lasdun for the re-development of the New Museums site was rejected by the planning authorities partly because it envisaged three towers, two of them 205 feet high, which would have radically altered the famous view of King's College Chapel and Gibb's Building as seen from the Backs. A third scheme put forward at a public enquiry in 1964 was still opposed; Denys Lasdun then retired, and Philip Dowson took over. As part of this scheme, laboratories for Mathematics and Zoology and a new Zoological Museum have been built.

In 1965 a committee chaired by Professor Deer considered plans for the science faculties for the next 20 years. It is planned to move biochemistry to the old Addenbrooke's site when this becomes available. It was recommended that physics should move to a site off Madingley Road, where other buildings, mainly for science, would eventually occupy a site of about 300 acres with buildings on 140.

The huge new Cavendish Laboratory, with wings bearing the illustrious names of Rutherford, Bragg and Mott, and costing £2.25 million, was opened there in 1973. It has been designed to be flexible; walls have been constructed so that they can be easily taken down and altered if necessary to meet changing requirements. The importance of Cambridge science was demonstrated on 27 February 1975, when ten Nobel prizewinners resident in the city attended a reception in the Guildhall.

The University Press acquired new buildings near the railway in 1961-3 at a cost of £1 million; all production areas are on a single level. The old press, except the Pitt Building, will eventually be demolished. The Local Examinations Syndicate offices arose on the old Perse School site in Hills Road in 1960-64. There was a need for a social centre for the increasing number of graduates and staff, and in 1964-67 the University

Centre, designed by Howell, Killick, Partridge and Amis, was erected in
Granta Place. The four-storey building has a large central cafeteria with a
fine open timber roof and skylight, also many common rooms and a more
luxurious dining room.

Every college has constructed additional buildings since the war. In
1937 Christ's rejected a design by Walter Gropius and Maxwell Fry,
and in 1948-50 and 1952-53 built two ranges designed by Sir Albert
Richardson and Eric Houfe which, with the earlier Stevenson building,
form a Third Court. Magdalene fortunately retained the old shops
opposite the main buildings of the college, and behind them, from 1952,
David Roberts adapted old buildings for college use and designed a
handsome three-storey building in yellow brick, also a four-storey block
near the river. In Benson Court the modern constructions and the diverse
old buildings co-exist happily side by side. Buckingham Court, built in
1968-69 in a bright red brick is visually less pleasing.

Trinity contrived a small court, Angel Court (1957-9), between the
shops in Trinity Street and the back of Great Court, and in 1959-60
Queens' put up the Erasmus Building, designed by Sir Basil Spence.
When the designs for this were published in 1958, there were many
protests, because Queens' retains more of its medieval buildings than any
other college, and people were alarmed at the prospect of a modern
building so close to them; in fact it blends admirably with the other
ranges in Friars' Court.

Harvey Court, designed by Sir Leslie Martin and Colin St John
Wilson, was built in West Road for Caius in 1960-62, and was at that
time the most striking new building of the colleges. Seen externally, there
are three sides of almost solid brick with few windows, and wide
buttresses supporting the top storey. Viewed from the south, open side, a
wide and imposing series of steps lead up from the garden to three
stepped tiers of rooms on terraces, with a breakfast room beneath in the
centre.

In 1960 the Trusted family, who were connected with Trinity Hall,
presented a new Garret Hostel Bridge to the city, a high-arched, graceful
structure with a concrete finish. In that year work began on the new
Addenbrooke's Hospital at Red Cross, which will eventually be the
largest and most expensive scheme undertaken in Cambridge since the
war.

Three new colleges, Churchill, Fitzwilliam and New Hall, have been built in close proximity between Huntingdon Road and Madingley Road, and it is perhaps unfortunate that a proposal of Peter Chamberlin in 1958 to co-ordinate the planning of them was not adopted. Churchill College was built as a national memorial to the great statesman at a cost of over £2½ million. It was planned to be unusually large, with over 500 students living-in and 60 Fellows, two-thirds of them scientists. A competition was won by Richard Sheppard, Robson and Partners, and building began in 1961. There are ten courts, some interlocking, of three storeys in brown brick and concrete, the smaller courts paved and others turfed. The rooms are spacious, with bay-windows in teak frames.

The Hall, seating 300, on an upper floor approached by a wide brick staircase, has a roof of three shell-concrete tunnel-vaults resting on massive concrete beams, covered externally with copper. The main end walls are elaborately panelled with red cedar-wood given by British Columbia. Beneath the Hall is a large combined bar and snack-bar. The free-standing Library group contains the long and high Bracken Library; at one end is a Jean Lurçat tapestry presented by de Gaulle. The Wolfson hall, seating 250, was designed for music, drama or meetings, and the Bevin reading room for postgraduates is on an upper floor. A recent addition is a building to contain the Winston Churchill archives. There are spacious playing-fields and a sports pavilion; a chapel, sited far from the main buildings after much controversy, some members being of the opinion that a chapel was unnecessary; and blocks of flats for research students and married graduates. Sculptures by Henry Moore and Barbara Hepworth adorn the grounds.

The university decided that Fitzwilliam Hall for students unattached to a college should be given full collegiate status. A site in Huntingdon Road was chosen, and the buildings were designed by Denys Lasdun and Partners. Construction began in 1961. Lasdun placed the Hall and Library near the centre, with residential ranges around them, forming two courts. There will eventually be a third court to the south. The Hall has striking clerestory windows, two common rooms are below the Library, and above another common room is a room seating 210 for music and drama.

For the first ten years after it was founded in 1954, the third college for women, New Hall, occupied The Hermitage in Silver Street. The

Darwin family presented a site in Huntingdon Road, and building began there in 1962. The architects, Chamberlin, Powell and Bon, have built in white brick. In the three-sided residential court, wide cloisters surround a pool. From the kitchen, a central hotplate rises on a lift to the Hall above, which is surmounted by a large dome with eight separate leaves. A Library, capable of containing 80,000 books, is placed on the west side of the court.

Newnham built an extension to the Library, designed by Lyster and Grillet, in 1961-62, and New Building, for 65 students, by the same architects in 1966-68, a Y-shaped building clad in pre-cast concrete panels with projecting windows. When Girton was founded, it was banished to the outskirts of the town, but the recent buildings have been erected in Clarkson Road.

Jesus has spacious grounds, and North Court, designed by David Roberts and erected in 1963-65, is sited beyond Outer Court. The rooms are placed diagonally to gain maximum light and privacy, and have large triangular balconies. Peterhouse, too, has ample space for new buildings, and the William Stone Building designed by Sir Leslie Martin and Colin St John Wilson was put up in 1963-64 at the southern end of the former deer park. This eight-storey block in brown brick is one of the best buildings of the 'sixties.

Another outstanding building is the Cripps Building of St. John's, designed by Powell and Moya, and erected in 1963-66 at a cost of £1 million. It forms two 3-sided courts stretching from the river to the School of Pythagoras; this late twelfth-century building has been renovated to form a large ground-floor area for entertaining, with a hall for music and drama above. The new ranges provide accommodation for 191 undergraduates, eight sets for Fellows, and a Junior Common Room. It is constructed with piers of reinforced concrete, with window mullions of white polished concrete and bronze window-frames. Bin Brook emerges from beneath the main building into a large punt lake near the river.

Corpus established a community for research students and bachelor Fellows at Leckhampton House off Grange Road and in 1963-64 put up a new building designed by Philip Dowson of Arup Associates. Two blocks of four and five storeys have a pre-cast concrete 'hanging frame' and large windows. It is one of the most attractive of the post-war

Cambridge buildings, and is placed in a mature garden of eight acres. The same firm designed somewhat similar buildings for Trinity Hall in the garden of 'Wychfield' in Huntingdon Road.

In 1965-68 King's and St Catharine's collaborated to sweep away some inferior buildings between the two colleges and erect five new courts designed by Fello Atkinson. This scheme has provided, for King's, 80 rooms for undergraduates, a new kitchen, concert hall, etc., and for St Catharine's 85 rooms, sets for seven Fellows, a new dining-hall, etc. This Hall has a large oriel facing Queens' Lane, a gallery, and is illuminated by four large low-slung steel chandeliers.

Three new colleges for graduates have been founded, the first, Darwin, in 1965, jointly by Caius, St John's and Trinity. It was accommodated in three houses in Silver Street, The Old Granary, Newnham Grange, and The Hermitage, and in 1966-68 two of these Victorian houses were linked by a building which enhances their appearance. An octagonal dining-hall on stilts to seat 140 was erected at the Newnham Terrace corner.

Clare, assisted by American benefactors, built Clare Hall in Herschel Road in 1966-69. The architect chosen was Ralph Erskine, and he grouped three houses, a block of houses and flats, looking southwards over the university football ground. The third graduate college, now called Wolfson, was founded by the university in 1965 in Bredon House in Barton Road, and is being extended.

For Selwyn, a large four-storey building to accommodate 130 undergraduates and about 40 graduates and Fellows was erected in Cranmer Road in 1966-68. Sidney has new buildings towards Malcolm Street begun in 1967, and Emmanuel built a second Hall and new kitchen in 1957-59, and two residential blocks in 1965-66.

Christ's accepted a design by Denys Lasdun in 1960 for a block on the King Street frontage, but building was delayed for five years by planning difficulties. Seen from the college grounds, there are tiers of stepped-back rooms, but the rear of the building in King Street looks like the back of a football stand.

A major project for Trinity, the Wolfson Building, is very fine but difficult to see as it is sited behind Sidney Street, Trinity Street, and Green Street. Seen from the air, it has been aptly described as 'looking like a liner in dry dock'. It is of five storeys with shops below. Queens'

are erecting a very large block, which includes a new Hall, on the wes
side of the river.

King's College Chapel was cleaned and restored internally in 1967-6
at a cost of £110,000. The grime from candle smoke was removed from
the walls and the wonderful fan-vaulted roof, underfloor heating wa
installed, and the marble paving at the east end relaid. It is expected tha
the interior will now remain clean for a considerable time, since smokeles
candles made of animal fat and imported from Sweden are now bein
used.

In 1961, Major A. E. Allnat gave to King's a large painting, *Th
Adoration of the Magi* by Rubens, which he had bought for £275,00(
This has been installed as an altar-piece, which necessitated the remova
of all of the Victorian panelling at this end of the Chapel, and the floc
had to be lowered. A new simple altar is covered with a clot
embroidered in colours blending with those in the painting. Electri
lighting has been installed for the first time, although candles are still use
during the services.

*   *   *

Cambridge is the main business and shopping centre for about 400,00(
persons, and all of the additional facilities required cannot b
accommodated in the historic central shopping area, which is no large
than it was in 1801 when the population of the city was a tenth of tha
today, and many surrounding villages show an even greater increase. /
second shopping centre on a site of 65 acres bounded by Maid"
Causeway, Newmarket Road, East Road, Parkside, and Emmanuel Roa(
was proposed, but this scheme would have necessitated the destruction o
many attractive Victorian houses. Several ambitious schemes for this are
were prepared, but all were rejected. The latest plans, on a smaller scale
for what is called the 'Fitzroy-Burleigh' area, are still being discussed.

A recent thorough survey conducted by a team under Professor Parr"
Lewis of Manchester University concluded that although the population
of the city has been controlled, the growth of the sub-regional population
increased mobility, and tourism, exert an ever-growing commercia
pressure on the historic centre. It is estimated that about two millio"
tourists come to Cambridge every year. If they were arranged in a queu

8 deep, it would stretch from King's Chapel to Marble Arch. Tourists spend about £10 million each year in the city shops and another £4·8 million on accommodation, though many come for only a few hours in coaches, which cause traffic and parking difficulties, and spend very little.

The population of the South Cambridgeshire area increased by 27% in the 'sixties, and it is estimated that the population of the city will increase by about 38,000 as a result of natural growth in the next 20 years. Professor Parry Lewis proposed that a second major centre should be built, preferably in the Trumpington area, to become comparable with the existing centre in about 20 years, and that then the population could rise from about 100,000 as at present to about 185,000.

This bold scheme would be very costly, and even if it were thought to be desirable, lack of resources would probably make it impossible within the time-scale contemplated. He also insisted that his plan would not be viable if the Fitzroy-Burleigh shopping area is developed. The planning authorities appear to feel that his proposals cannot be accepted.

The main proposal in a very detailed Transportation Study was for a new relief road to run through the city beside the railway but this has been rejected as it is estimated that it would cost £10 million, i.e., all the available funds for roads for the next 15 years. In the meantime the traffic situation becomes daily more acute; numerous huge container lorries pass through the city as they travel between the Midlands and the East Coast ports. The recent construction of Elizabeth Way and a new bridge over the river came only just in time to save the situation. A public enquiry into proposals for two by-passes for the city had to consider nearly 120 objections and lasted for almost six months. A long time elapsed before the Minister gave a decision in favour of constructing them, and work on one has now begun.

By comparison with many other towns, only a small part of the central area has been freed from traffic. Vehicles have been banished from Petty Cury and the Lion Yard Development, and motor traffic except buses and taxis from parts of King's Parade, Sidney Street, and St Andrew's Street. Eventually it is hoped to extend this scheme, and restrict traffic along Queen's Road.

During the past 25 years, many plans for the future of the city have been made, exhaustively discussed, and finally abandoned. Cambridge has so many intelligent and articulate people that every plan has caused endless argument, and Government decisions are always slow presumably because Ministers are aware that Cambridge is a unique city and they hesitate to make decisions which future generations might condemn.

The size of the university increases year by year, but it has been decided that only a modest number of additional students will be admitted in the next few years. There are now about 9,000 undergraduates, plus about 2,500 graduates doing advanced work or research. Some graduates from other universities come for two years to take a Cambridge B. A. Degree, others stay for three years to gain a doctorate. Standards for acceptance are high; about 40% of those admitted have three 'A' Levels or more, compared with about 9% at other universities other than Oxford. There is a very large teaching and administrative staff, and many hundreds of people work in the scientific laboratories; in the university, faculty, and college libraries; in museums or in the colleges as clerks, cooks, gardeners, etc.

The age of entry is usually 19-20, and there are still about six times as many men as women. The reader should not conclude from these figures that the male students are deprived of girl friends. Since the war numerous schools teaching English to foreigners (mostly female) have been established in the city, and there are the students at Homerton, a training college for teachers, at the Technical College, and the nurses of Addenbrooke's Hospital.

Three of the men's colleges, King's, Clare and Churchill, now admit a small number of girls, and some other colleges will probably do so in the future. Owing to the scarcity of places for girls, only one of every four or five who apply can be accepted, compared with about half of the men. The first female Vice-Chancellor took office in October 1975.

There has been a certain amount of student unrest, but not as serious as elsewhere. Some of the disciplinary measures have been relaxed, and students are represented on faculty boards and other bodies. Most of them probably work harder than their predecessors, and one result of this is that fewer take part in sport, and standards have fallen, though the 1975-6 rugger team was outstanding. 130 boats compete in the May Races; the Lady Margaret (St John's) club has 13 eights and Trinity has 10.

Academics are now not so clearly distinguishable from townsfolk as formerly, when dons strode through the streets in long gowns and mortar-boards, and hundreds of students wearing both hurried to and from lectures on bicycles. Gowns are more rarely worn, and the 'square' went out of use in the Second World War. Formerly, the city was noticeably less crowded during the vacations, but colleges now accommodate people attending conferences of all kinds at these times.

The central streets become more congested with vehicles and pedestrians year by year, but one can still pass through college gateways into courts which are comparatively peaceful, and which have not changed greatly since Milton, Byron, Newton, Darwin, Pepys or Cromwell and a host of other famous men walked in them. The Backs are somewhat disfigured by hundreds of parked cars and an endless stream of traffic in Queen's Road, but when the by-passes have been constructed it is intended to restrict traffic there. With the present and future university and college buildings to the west of it, the area on both sides of Queen's Road may become the largest and finest campus in the world.

Select
Bibliography

Atkinson, T. D., and Clark, J. W., Cambridge Described and Illustrated (1897)

Bonney, T. G., A Septuagenarian's Recollections of St. John's (1909)

Booth, P. and Taylor, N., Cambridge New Architecture (1970)

Browning, O., Memories of 60 Years (1910)

Bushell, W. D., The Church of St Mary the Great (1948)
Hobson's Conduit (1938)

Clark, J. W. Cambridge. Brief Historical and Picturesque Notes (1890)
Memories and Customs, 1820-1860 (1909)
and Gray, A. Old Plans of Cambridge, 1574 to 1798 (1921)

Cooper, C. H., Annals of Cambridge, (4 vols. 1842-52. Vol. 5 1908)

Everett, W. On the Cam. Lectures on the University of Cambridge (1866)

Fawcett, M. G. What I Remember (1924)

Gray, A., Cambridge Revisited (1921)
The Town of Cambridge (1925)
Cambridge University: an Episodical History (1926)

Gunning, H., Selections from Gunning's Reminiscences of Cambridge (1932)

Heitland, W. E., After Many Years (1926)

Holford, W. and Wright, H. Myles. Cambridge Planning Proposals (1950)

Jebb, E. Cambridge, A Brief Study in Social Questions (1906)

Le Keux, J. Memorials of Cambridge (New edition by C. H. Cooper, 1860-66)

Lobel, M. D., Cambridge (1974)

Merivale, C., Autobiography and Letters (1898)

Moorman, J. R. H., The Grey Friars in Cambridge 1225-1538 (1952)

Morgan, H. A., Memoirs (1927)

Pevsner, Sir N., The Buildings of England: Cambridgeshire (1954)

Rait, R. S. Life in the Medieval University (1931)

Raverat, G., Period Piece. A Cambridge Childhood (1952)

Roberts, Sir S. C., Introduction to Cambridge (1934)

Royal Commission on Historical Monuments, City of Cambridge (1959)

Smith, J. J., The Cambridge Portfolio (1840)

Stephen, B. Girton College 1869-1932 (1933)

Stuart, J. Reminiscences (1862)

Thomson, Sir J. J., Recollections and Reflections (1936)

Varley, F. J., Cambridge During the Civil War 1642-1646 (1935)

Venn, J. Early Collegiate Life (1913)

Victoria History of the Counties of England, Cambridge, Vol. 3: The
City and University of Cambridge (1959)

White, R. J., Dr. Bentley (1965)
Cambridge Life (1960)

Widnall, S. P., A Gossiping Stroll Through the Streets of Cambridge
(1892)

Willis, R., and Clark, J. W., The Architectural History of the University
of Cambridge (1886)

Winstanley, D. A., The University of Cambridge in the Eighteenth
Century (1922)
Unreformed Cambridge (1935)
Early Victorian Cambridge (1940)
Later Victorian Cambridge (1947)

Index